Colette's Cakes

Colette's Cakes

The Art of Cake Decorating

COLETTE PETERS

LITTLE, BROWN AND COMPANY

Boston   New York   London

FIRST EDITION

Photographs by Deborah Klesenski and Bob Ward, with additional photographs by
Lynne Reynolds appearing on pages 65, 80, 94, 131, 134, 153, and 156.
Illustrated by Colette Peters and Anne Russinof.

LIBRARY OF CONGRESS CATALOGING-IN-PUBLICATION DATA
Peters, Colette.
Colette's cakes : the art of cake decorating / by Colette Peters.
p.   cm.
Includes index.
ISBN 0-316-70205-6
1. Cake decorating. I. Title.
TX771.P47   1991
641.8'653—dc20   90-24676

10   9   8   7

IP

Designed by Barbara Werden

PRINTED IN HONG KONG

To Aunt Rose, for your lamb cakes.

Contents

Introduction

I've always loved making cakes. As a child I used to help my mom in the kitchen to see what kind of concoctions I could come up with. Later, I started making cakes for my friends, and each time I decided to make a cake, I wanted it to be more creative and more of a challenge than the last one. I began buying some books on cake decorating to learn the basics, and then I started to make up my own techniques.

Working as an artist in New York City has helped me to develop my sense of design and to expand my cake-decorating horizons. It also gave me an abundance of visual resources for new ideas. Parts II, III, and IV contain some of the ideas and designs I have developed throughout the years.

This book is not intended to be a cookbook, although Part I does contain all of the necessary recipes for creating the cakes in the book. The sections on servings (page 26) and flowers (pages 15–24) give you an idea of how much of the various cakes and icings you will need. Experience and experimentation will also help to determine this. "Tools of the Trade" is a guide to supplies needed to decorate almost any cake.

The book begins with cakes a beginner can make and progresses to some that only a very patient person will attempt. But the more complicated cakes can be made on a smaller scale to help you gain confidence so that you can eventually create cakes on a larger scale. I hope that you can come up with some of your own ideas, and that this book will be an inspiration to invent your own creative cakes.

Part
I

Getting
Started

1

Tools of the Trade

There are many specialized items available for the cake decorator, but chances are you already have many of the basic tools in your home. The following list contains most of the items you will need to decorate the cakes in this book. Don't go out and buy everything at once; purchase things as you need them.

ALUMINUM FOIL, WAXED PAPER, and PLASTIC WRAP
  COUPLERS: Plastic couplers fit inside the pastry bag and the decorating tip fits on top. The tip is then secured in place with a threaded ring (Figure 1). Couplers allow easy tip-changing without having to change bags. All decorating tips, except for the very small or very large, fit onto the couplers.

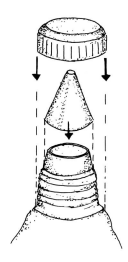

Figure 1

CUTTERS: GUM PASTE, COOKIE, and BISCUIT: Gum paste cutters are specifically designed for making a variety of flowers in gum paste and can be purchased from cake-decorating stores.

CUTTING BOARD, PLASTIC or MARBLE: For making gum paste decorations. A rubber placemat can also be used.

DECORATING TIPS: There are hundreds of tips to choose from, but to start decorating, you can buy a beginner set of various tips and then buy additional tips as needed.

¼-INCH WOODEN DOWELS or PLASTIC DRINKING STRAWS: Dowels can be bought at a hardware store or an art supply store. They are used as a support for multiple tiers.

DRAGEES: Silver- or gold-covered candy balls, which come in various sizes. They are completely edible and can add sparkle to your cake.

FLOWER NAILS: Flat or cupped supports on which flowers are piped. These can be found at cake-decorating stores.

FOAM BOARD: Foam board is a thin piece of Styrofoam sandwiched between two pieces of thin white cardboard. I use these to make my cake bases and as supports between multiple tiers. Foam board has much more strength and does not bend as easily as corrugated cardboard.

FOOD COLORING: Food coloring comes in several forms — paste, liquid, and powder. The paste form is the most versatile. This is a highly concentrated coloring and a little dab on the end of a toothpick is usually all you need. *Paste* food coloring can be found in cake-decorating supply stores. *Liquid* food colors commonly found in the grocery store can come in handy. However, to make the icing a dark color, you must add large amounts, which will thin the icing too much, making piping difficult. *Powdered* food colors are completely edible and are used for making metallic and iridescent effects, or for making very deep colors. Icing flowers can also be dusted with powders, using a small brush, to give them a more realistic look. Powdered colors can also be made into a paint by adding a little bit of lemon extract and applying to rolled fondant, royal icing, or gum paste with a paintbrush.

HEAVY-DUTY MIXER: For the occasional baker, a regular upright mixer is fine, but if you are going to be doing a substantial amount of decorating, a heavy-duty mixer is best. Hand-held mixers tend to burn out and are not very efficient.

PAINTBRUSHES: Small round, soft paintbrushes and large pastry brushes come in very handy for many decorating uses.

PASTRY BAGS: The best type of bag is made of lightweight polyester. Cloth bags are bulky and hard to clean thoroughly. Buy a few bags and keep the ones you use for royal icing separate from those for buttercream. The fat from the buttercream will break down royal icing, even if the bag is very thoroughly cleaned. I have found that the 10-inch bag is the easiest to work with.

PASTRY CLOTH: Any clean white cotton cloth can be used for rolling out fondant.

PRUNING SHEARS: These are used to trim your dowels.

ROLLING PIN: A large rolling pin is essential for rolling out fondant, but a small one is good for rolling out gum paste decorations.

RULER, 18-INCH METAL

SCISSORS

SPATULA: A stainless-steel spatula is an absolute necessity. The one that I use most is an 8-inch angled spatula. Also, a plastic icing smoother is a great aid when icing large cakes. These can be found in a hardware store in the spackling section.

STAMENS: These can be found in cake-decorating stores or florist shops. A stamen consists of a thin piece of stiff thread with a tiny pearlized ball on each end. They are cut in half and then inserted into the center of your icing flower while the icing is still soft. They come in a variety of colors and sizes and should not be eaten.

ROUND TOOTHPICKS: To make stems for flowers and for adding paste colors to icing. Also used as a tool for embossing fondant.

TAPE, FLORIST: Tape used to cover wires and to bind multiple wired flowers together. It comes in white, green, and brown and can be found at flower shops and cake-decorating suppliers.

TURNTABLE: This is an invaluable tool that will make a cake decorator's life much easier. You don't have to buy an expensive turntable; a plastic one found in most hardware stores used for storing spices is fine and will support the heaviest cake.

TWEEZERS: Makes picking up dragees and stamens easier.

WIRES, CLOTH-COVERED: Found in florist shops and cake-decorating stores, these come in white or green and a variety of thicknesses.

X-ACTO KNIFE: I use an X-acto knife with the long pointed blade. It has a thin metal handle and a blade which screws into the handle and can be changed easily. You will need a lot of extra blades, since they tend to dull quickly.

Recipes

Colette's Chocolate Cake

This is a deliciously rich cake that's moist and very easy to make. It's the most popular cake that I make.

2 cups sugar
2 eggs, room temperature
1 cup milk, room temperature
1 cup unsweetened cocoa
1 cup vegetable shortening or butter, softened
1 teaspoon salt
2 teaspoons baking powder
1 teaspoon baking soda
1 teaspoon almond extract
1 teaspoon vanilla extract
2½ cups all-purpose flour
1¼ cup hot, strong coffee

Pre-heat the oven to 325 degrees F. Grease the sides and bottom of the cake pans with shortening and then dust with flour.

In a large mixing bowl, combine all the ingredients except the coffee. Mix at low speed until all the ingredients are blended, scraping the sides occasionally with a rubber spatula. Slowly add the coffee while mixing on slow. Mix until smooth. Bake for about 35 minutes or until a toothpick inserted in the center comes out clean. Cool in the pans for about 20 minutes, then invert onto racks and remove the

pans. Cool completely before icing. Yields 6 cups of batter, enough to serve 20.

Snow White Cake

This is pure white cake that's light and not too sweet.

¾ cup Crisco or vegetable shortening
1½ cups sugar
2 teaspoons vanilla extract
2¾ cups sifted cake flour
½ teaspoon salt
4 teaspoons baking powder
1 cup milk, room temperature
4 egg whites, room temperature

Pre-heat the oven to 350 degrees F. Grease and then flour the sides and bottom of the cake pans.

In a large bowl of an electric mixer, cream the shortening until light and airy. Slowly add 1 cup of sugar, continually beating until fluffy. Add the vanilla.

In a small bowl, sift the dry ingredients together. Add 1 tablespoon of the dry ingredients to the shortening mixture and mix well. Then, add 1 tablespoon of milk to the shortening mixture and mix well. Continue adding these ingredients, alternating and mixing well after each addition until all of the ingredients have been combined.

In another bowl, beat the egg whites until fluffy. Slowly add ½ cup of sugar and beat until stiff, shiny peaks form. Gently fold the egg whites into the batter mixture until blended, being careful not to overmix. Place in the prepared pans. Bake about 20 minutes or until toothpick inserted into center of cake comes out clean. Let the cakes cool in the pans for about 20 minutes, then invert onto wire racks and remove the pans. Cool completely. Yields 6 cups, enough to serve 20.

Basic Buttercream Icing

This is a very easy icing to make and is good for icing a cake or for piping decorations and borders. It will stay fresh for two days without refrigeration.

  1 cup unsalted butter or margarine, room
      temperature (use vegetable shortening when
      pure white icing is needed)
  ½ cup milk, room temperature
  ¼ teaspoon salt
  2 teaspoons vanilla or other desired flavoring
  2 pounds confectioner's sugar

Combine all the ingredients in large mixing bowl and mix at slow speed until smooth. If stiffer icing is needed, or the weather is very warm, add a little extra sugar. This recipe is enough to cover and fill a 9x13-inch sheet cake or two 9-inch layers. Yields 6 cups.

Meringue Buttercream

This is a deliciously light and airy icing that is good for covering and filling a cake. It has a lighter taste than basic buttercream, but is somewhat more complicated to make. It is not recommended for use in very hot and humid weather.

  2 cups softened unsalted butter
  1 cup granulated sugar
  ¼ cup water
  5 large egg whites, room temperature
  ½ teaspoon cream of tartar
  2 teaspoons flavoring or liqueur
  candy thermometer

Beat the butter until smooth and set aside. In a small saucepan, add the water and ¾ cup of sugar. Stir until the sugar is dissolved. Slowly heat the mixture while constantly stirring until it starts to bubble. Reduce heat to low and insert a candy thermometer. Do not stir the sugar anymore.

In a large bowl of an electric mixer, beat the egg whites at low speed until foamy. Add cream of tartar and beat at high speed until peaks form. Gradually add the ¼ cup sugar until stiff peaks form.

Meanwhile, boil the sugar mixture until it reaches 250 degrees on the candy thermometer. When this temperature is reached, turn off the heat and pour the contents into a glass measuring cup to stop the sugar from cooking. Slowly pour the sugar mixture onto the egg whites, beating on low until all of the sugar is added. Then beat at medium speed until the mixture is cool.

Add the butter, one tablespoon at a time, to the egg white mixture, continually beating until all of the butter is added. Beat until smooth, then add the flavoring. This icing will keep at room temperature for two days or refrigerated for ten days. This is enough icing to fill and cover a two-layer 9-inch cake. Yields 4½ cups.

Rolled Fondant

Rolled fondant is a very tasty and smooth icing that is rolled out with a rolling pin, draped over the cake, and smoothed down with the hands. British cake decorators have traditionally used fondant and now it has become very popular in the United States. Rolled fondant gives a cake a beautiful porcelain-like surface on which to decorate. Pre-made fondant can also be purchased from cake-decorating suppliers and works very well.

> 2 pounds confectioner's sugar, sifted
> ¼ cup cold water
> 1 tablespoon unflavored gelatin
> ½ cup glucose (found in cake-decorating stores), or white corn syrup
> 1½ tablespoons glycerine (found in cake-decorating stores)
> 1 teaspoon desired flavoring (vanilla will give the fondant an off-white color)
> cornstarch

In a large bowl (do not use metal), sift the sugar and make a well in the center. In a small saucepan, add the water and sprinkle the gelatin on top to soften for about 5 minutes. Begin to heat the gelatin and stir until the gelatin is dissolved and clear. Do not boil. Turn off the heat and add the glucose and glycerine, stirring until well blended. Add the flavoring. Pour into the well of sugar, and mix until all of the sugar is blended. Use hands to knead icing until it becomes stiff. Add small amounts of confectioner's sugar if the mixture is sticky.

Form the mixture into a ball and wrap tightly in plastic wrap. Place in an airtight container. This icing works best if allowed to rest at room temperature for about eight hours before using, particularly if the weather is humid. Do not refrigerate fondant.

To cover a cake with fondant:

Dust a clean pastry cloth, or a smooth, clean surface, with cornstarch and roll the fondant with a rolling pin until it is approximately ¼ inch thick. Make sure that the fondant is large enough to fit over the top and sides of the cake. Slide both hands under the fondant and carefully center it on top of a cake that has been freshly iced with buttercream. (The icing makes the fondant adhere to the cake.)

Dust your hands with cornstarch and smooth the fondant, starting at the top and working down the sides until the entire surface is even and flat (Figure 1). Cut off the excess icing around the bottom of the cake with a pizza cutter or sharp knife (Figure 2). Decorate the cake with buttercream or royal icing. This fondant keeps a cake fresh for two days at room temperature. Do not refrigerate a cake with rolled fondant icing. Yields enough icing to cover a 9-inch cake, 4 inches high.

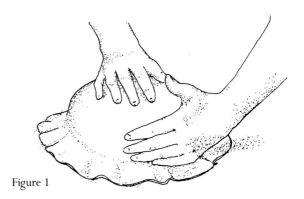

Figure 1

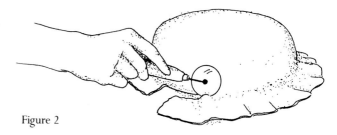

Figure 2

Royal Icing

This is a pure white decorative icing that dries very hard. It is perfect for making flowers and bows and can be kept in an airtight container at room temperature for two weeks. Stir icing with a spatula to restore its consistency. Do not rebeat. Royal icing does not stand up to high humidity.

> 5 tablespoons meringue powder (found in cake-decorating stores) *or* 2 room-temperature egg whites can be substituted for the meringue powder and the water
> ½ cup minus 2 tablespoons water
> ½ teaspoon cream of tartar
> a few drops of colorless flavoring (pure vanilla is good for an off-white color)
> 1 pound confectioner's sugar

Place all of the ingredients in the bowl of an electric mixer. Beat slowly until all of the ingredients are blended. Then, beat at high speed until icing forms stiff peaks, about 5 minutes. Add more sugar if the icing is not stiff enough, or a few drops of water if it is too stiff. Use immediately, or cover the bowl with a damp cloth to prevent drying when not in use. Allow at least twenty-four hours for royal icing decorations to dry at room temperature. Yields 3 cups.

Run-in Sugar

Run-in sugar is simply royal icing that has been thinned with water until it has a "runny" consistency. It is then piped through a thin tip into a shape that has been outlined on waxed paper with stiff royal icing. The run-in sugar fills in the shape and dries to a very hard consistency.

Run-in sugar decorations can be used for making shapes on wires simply by laying the wire on the waxed paper in the center of the design and outlining and filling in the design with the wire in place. The icing will dry with the wire tightly locked into the shape. It is a good idea to go back and fill in the back of the design again when the front has dried, which gives the wired shape more strength.

To make run-in sugar designs:

Place the pattern you want to reproduce in sugar on a flat surface. Tape a piece of waxed paper on top of the pattern. Outline the design on the waxed paper with stiff royal icing, using the #3 tip. Place some stiff royal icing in a bowl and add a few drops of water while continually stirring. Continue adding water, a few drops at a time, until a teaspoon full of icing dropped into the bowl disappears into the rest of the icing on the count of ten. It should have the consistency of corn syrup. Pipe the run-in sugar into the outlined design with a #2 tip, filling in the entire shape up to the outline (Figure 3). Allow run-in sugar designs to dry for at

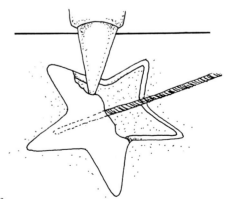

Figure 3

least twenty-four hours. Repeat on the other side when the first side is dry. Slip a metal spatula under the design to remove it from the waxed paper. (Hint: when using two or more colors in a run-in design, allow the first color to dry before adding the second color. This will prevent the colors from bleeding into one another.)

Gum Paste

Gum paste is an edible modeling material perfect for making realistic flowers and bows. It can be rolled very thin and when dry, is very hard, similar to porcelain. It can be tinted with paste food coloring and brushed with edible colored powders. When kneaded with an equal amount of rolled fondant, it also makes beautiful ruffles and roses.

> 1 cup "Country Kitchen" gum paste mix (available in cake-decorating stores)
> 1 tablespoon hot water

Use a nonmetal bowl when making gum paste, as a metal bowl may turn the paste gray. Mix ½ cup of the gum paste with the water. When thoroughly blended, add the remaining gum paste mix and work with your hands until it forms a solid mass. Add small amounts of the dry mix if the paste is still sticky. Form the mixture into a ball and rub the surface with a little vegetable shortening. Place in a plastic bag and seal with all of the air squeezed out. Place the bag in an airtight container for at least twenty-four hours at room temperature. This gives the paste time to set. It will keep at room temperature for two weeks, but should be kneaded occasionally to restore its consistency. If longer storage is necessary, refrigerate the paste for up to three weeks. (Allow the gum paste to return to room temperature before using.)

To make sure that the paste has the proper consistency when ready to use, pull the paste apart. It should "snap" when pulled apart. If it does not snap, knead in some of the dry gum paste mixture until it reaches the proper consistency.

Sugar Molds

Molding a form in sugar is an easy way to make edible decorations or vases to hold sugar flowers for the top of a cake. Any smooth metal, plastic, or glass cup, bowl, or container can be used as your form for the mold. You probably have many containers in your home that will work quite well. The only thing to remember when looking for the appropriate container is that the top of the form should be wider than the bottom, or the sugar will not come out of the form. Sugar molds dry very hard and can be hollowed out before they are completely dry to make the mold more lightweight.

> 1 tablespoon cold water
> 1 cup granulated sugar

This recipe is enough to make a small mold, but if you are making something large, you will need to know how much sugar to use. Since dry sugar takes up more space than wet sugar, first fill the container twice with dry sugar and pour it into a bowl. Measure the amount of sugar in the bowl and this will tell you how much water is needed. (Add 1 tablespoon of water to each cup of sugar.)

If you want to make a colored sugar mold, add some food coloring to the water before adding the water to the dry sugar.

Add the water to the sugar in a glass or plastic bowl. Mix with your hand until all of the sugar is damp. Using your hand is messy, but it makes it easier to tell if the sugar is thoroughly mixed. Pack the sugar tightly into the clean container, pressing firmly with your hand. Even off the top with a knife and invert onto a piece of waxed paper. Gently lift off the container. If the sugar doesn't come out of the container, pick it up and turn it over again, tapping the container. Let the sugar mold set overnight, upside down.

After the mold has set overnight, you can hollow it out by carefully turning the mold right side up and scooping out the still damp sugar with a spoon. Be careful not to make the sides of the mold too thin, since the mold is not completely dry yet and could break. Then allow the mold to dry completely, right side up, for at least twenty-four hours.

3

Basic Cake-Decorating Techniques

Tips on Icing a Cake

One of the hardest techniques for the cake decorator to master is icing a cake smoothly. If a cake is to be covered with rolled fondant, the icing layer on the cake does not have to be perfectly smooth, since it will not be visible. If the cake is to be covered only with buttercream icing, the surface should be as smooth as possible to give a professional look. Using a turntable is a must when icing round layers, but it makes icing any shape a lot easier.

First, place the filling between the layers or, if you have only a single layer, slice the cake in half, horizontally, with a serrated knife. Remove the top and add the filling, then replace the top half and press the top of the cake gently with your hands to make sure that the cake is settled as much as possible. Let the cake sit for an hour before icing to make sure the filling has set. This will insure that the icing on the cake does not buckle between the layers after it is iced.

Next, ice the cake with a thin coat of icing to set the crumbs. Add a few drops of water to the icing to thin it slightly. Use a metal spatula and ice as smoothly as possible.

A second coating of icing is then added after the first coat is dry. This should be a thicker coating to cover any imperfections in the first coat. It is easier to get a smooth surface if the icing is slightly soft. Add a few drops of water to the icing. If you are using meringue buttercream, do not thin the icing with water. Meringue buttercream smooths easier than basic buttercream, but you can dip your spatula in hot water and shake off the excess water. The hot metal will smooth the icing nicely.

Ice the sides of the cake first and then the top, to smooth the icing over the edges of the sides and onto the top.

A quick technique I have learned from fellow cake decorators to give the cake a smooth appearance is to take an untextured paper towel and lay it on the cake after the coat of icing is dry to the touch and smooth the towel lightly with your hands. This will smooth out any imperfections in the icing. A textured paper towel can be used to add an interesting pattern to the surface of the cake.

Piping Techniques

There are many piping techniques used in cake decorating that can turn a simple cake into something spectacular. Once you have learned the basics, you can combine different techniques and invent some of your own.

The piping is done directly on the cake with buttercream or royal icing. Buttercream icing is usually piped on a buttercream-covered cake, while royal icing is generally piped on a fondant-covered cake. However, buttercream icing can also be successfully piped onto fondant, and royal icing decorations can be added to any type of cake.

Borders

There are as many border designs as there are decorating tips. A border around the bottom edges of your cake will give it a professional finish.

DOT BORDER: Dots are made with a round tip. These vary in size, starting with the smallest tip, #1, up to #12. After determining the size of the border desired, pick the appropriate-sized tip. Hold the tip perpendicular to the cake and apply pressure to the pastry bag. Squeeze until the dot is the size you wish. Slowly pull the tip away from the dot with a slight swirling motion, so that the dot does not end in a point.

SHELL BORDER: Shell borders are made with a star tip, #13 to #32. Other star tips are available, but these are the most commonly used. The tip is held at a slight angle from the cake. Start applying pressure to the bag and move the tip slightly away from you. Then, as the icing starts to flow from the bag, move the tip up, apply more pressure to the pastry bag, and then move the tip down. End the shell in a point. Start the next shell on top of the point of the first shell (Figure 1).

STAR BORDER: The star border is made in the same way as the dot border, but with a star tip. Hold the tip perpendicular to the cake and apply pressure. Pull away from the cake when the desired-sized star is made (Figure 2).

Figure 2

DROP STRINGS: Strings of icing are piped with a round tip. The string of icing actually drops down in an arch while you apply pressure to the bag. This technique should be practiced before trying it on an actual cake. First, evenly spaced marks should be made on the cake so that you will know where to begin and end your string, and how long to make the string. Place the tip against the first mark and start applying pressure to the bag. The icing will adhere to the cake. Pull the tip away from the cake while still applying pressure to the bag and allowing the icing to flow. Gravity will make the icing drop in a curve. Let enough icing out of the tip to reach the next mark (Figure 3). Make all of the strings the same length.

Figure 3

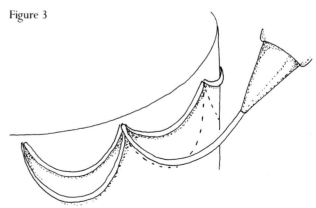

Figure 1

You can vary your drop strings by using multiple strings or overlapping strings. The icing should be of a slightly soft consistency, to help insure that the strings will not break. If using royal icing, let the icing set for a day in an airtight container before piping. This allows the icing to settle so that there won't be any air bubbles to break the strings while you are working.

LEAVES: Leaves are generally piped directly on the cake with buttercream icing. Flowers are attached to the cake with a mound of buttercream and then leaves are piped around the base of the flowers. Leaf tips vary in size, from #65 to #70 and #352. The #352 tip is good for making leaves that will always end in a point as the other tips will sometimes leave the end in a notch. A leaf can be smooth or ruffled, depending on how much pressure is applied to the pastry bag.

Figure 4

ZIGZAGS: The zigzag line is made with a star tip. While applying pressure to the bag, move the tip up and down so that each line of icing is touching the one before it (Figure 4).

Marking Divisions on a Cake for Decorating

When you plan to decorate a cake with a regular pattern on the sides or top, you need to place marks on the cake as a guide to where to add your decorations. Your cake will have a much more professional look if your decorations are pre-planned and evenly spaced.

A simple way to find the center of a cake is with a piece of paper cut to the size of the cake. To find the center of a round cake, trace the bottom of the pan in which the cake was baked onto a piece of paper. Cut out the outline of the pan. Fold the paper in half. Then fold the paper again into quarters (Figure 5).

Figure 5

Open the paper and mark the center of the circle with a toothpick hole. Place the paper on the top of the cake and mark the cake with a toothpick through the center of the paper. You can follow the same procedure for a square or rectangular cake.

To divide a cake into eighths or sixteenths, use the same steps as above, but fold the paper once more (eighths) or twice more (sixteenths) (Figure 6). Open the paper and place it on the top of the cake. Mark the cake with a toothpick at the folds on the paper (Figure 7).

If you want to divide the cake into a different number of divisions, you will have to use a protractor to find the correct angle on which to fold your paper.

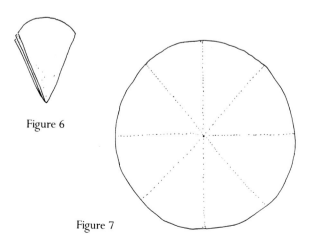

Figure 6

Figure 7

4

Royal Icing Decorations

Flowers in Royal Icing

All of the flowers in this book, except for the peony and the quick rose, are made in royal icing. Once you know the basic techniques, almost any flower can be made in icing. Royal icing dries very hard; therefore, icing flowers can last a long time if kept in a covered container at room temperature. The icing should be of a stiff consistency when piping flowers.

Flower nails are needed to make most flowers. Flower nails come in different sizes, but the #7 flower nail and the large lily nail are the most commonly used. The nail is held in one hand and turned while piping with the other hand.

The basic flower nail is a long metal stick with a round, flat surface on top (Figure 1). This nail is used to make daisies, roses, carnations, and other flat-bottomed flowers. Waxed paper squares are attached to the nail with a dab of icing and the flower is piped onto the waxed paper.

The lily nail has a cupped surface and is used to make lilies, poinsettias, petunias, and other cupped flowers (Figure 2). Foil squares are pressed into the nail and folded around the edges. The flower is piped onto the foil and set aside to dry. The flower will then release easily

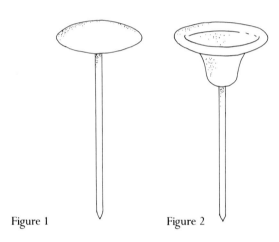

Figure 1   Figure 2

from the foil. (Hint: These flowers take longer to dry than flat flowers.)

To color flowers in royal icing, the centers or edges of the petals can be dusted with powdered food colors with a small paintbrush to give a more realistic look. Use powders only on a completely dry flower.

Another way to vary the coloring of the flower is to paint a stripe of paste coloring inside the bag before filling it with icing. Paint the stripe along the seam of the bag to keep track of where the color is. The icing will come out of the bag in a two-color stripe.

You can also achieve a striped effect by filling the length of the bag with two different colors of icing. When the icing is piped out of the bag, the petals will have a two-tone look.

Flowers Made on the Flower Nail

The directions for the flowers below list basic tip sizes. You can vary the size of the tip to get larger or smaller flowers.

THE DAISY
tips #5; #102 or #103
2-inch waxed paper squares
granulated sugar

Daisies come in a wide variety of colors but are most commonly made with white petals and a yellow center. Attach a waxed paper square to the nail with a dab of icing. Fill a pastry bag with white royal icing and attach a #102 or #103 tip. Hold the nail in your left hand and the pastry bag in your right (if left-handed, do the opposite). Place the wide end of the tip at the center of the paper and start piping, moving the tip out toward the edge of the paper, then back toward the center again (Figure 3). Begin and end each petal in the center. Turn the nail after each petal. Make five petals.

To make the center of the flower, the daisy must be dry. Pipe a #5 dot in the center of the flower and sprinkle with granulated sugar (Figure 4).

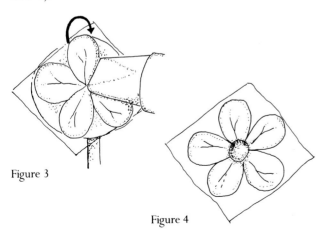

Figure 3

Figure 4

THE DOUBLE-LAYERED DAISY
tips #102, #104
3-inch waxed paper squares
stamens

Attach the waxed paper square to the nail with a dab of icing. Pipe seven large petals with the #104 tip, in the same manner as the daisy (Figure 5). Pipe six smaller petals inside the large petals with the #102 tip (Figure 6). Insert ten stamens.

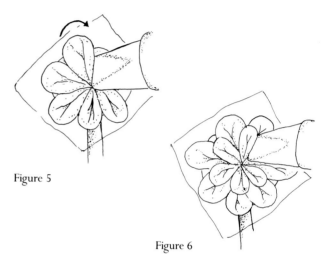

Figure 5

Figure 6

THE ROSE
tips #9, #102, #103, or #104
2-inch waxed paper squares

On a sheet of waxed paper, pipe large white cones with the #9 tip. Pipe as many cones as needed. Let the cones dry completely.

Place a 2-inch square of waxed paper on a flower nail with a dab of icing. Place a cone on the paper with a dab of icing (Figure 7). Depending on the size of the rose, fit a #102, #103, or #104 tip onto the pastry bag. Place the wide end of the tip at the base of the cone, with the narrow end facing up. Start piping around the cone, moving the tip up and then down while turning the nail counterclockwise with the other hand. Stop piping when you

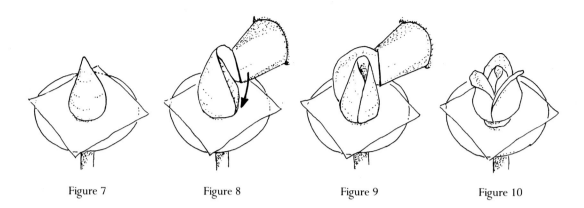

Figure 7   Figure 8   Figure 9   Figure 10

reach the place that you started. You can stop here if you only want a rose bud (Figure 8).

Pipe three petals around the bud, applying more pressure to the bag and holding the narrow end of the tip slightly away from the bud. Move the tip up and then down to form the petals (Figures 9 and 10).

Add four larger petals, starting and ending at the center of the previous three petals (Figure 11).

Add six larger petals around the rose to finish (Figure 12).

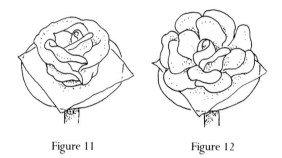

Figure 11   Figure 12

THE CARNATION
tip #102
2-inch waxed paper squares

Attach the waxed paper to the nail with a dab of icing. Place the wide end of the #102 tip against the center of the waxed paper square. Start piping the first petal by moving the tip straight out toward the edge and then back to the center so that the end of the petal folds slightly onto itself (Figure 13). Pipe nine petals (Figure 14). Continue the same procedure, piping eight smaller petals by using less pressure on the bag, between the previous petals (Figure 15). Pipe seven smaller petals on top of the previous petals (Figure 16).

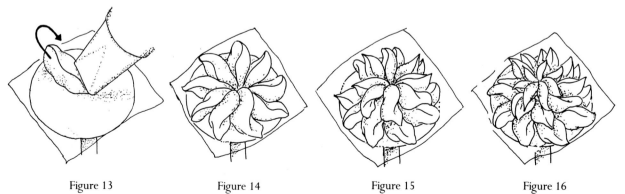

Figure 13   Figure 14   Figure 15   Figure 16

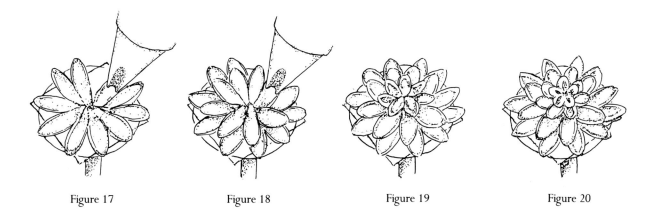

Figure 17   Figure 18   Figure 19   Figure 20

THE CHRYSANTHEMUM
tip #80
2-inch waxed paper squares

Attach the waxed paper square to the nail with a dab of icing. Place the tip in the center of the waxed paper square with the round edge of the tip against the paper. Pipe a line of icing out to the edge of the nail. Pipe petals all around the nail (Figure 17).

Pipe another row of shorter petals on top of the first row (Figure 18). Pipe a third row of shorter petals on top of the second row (Figure 19). Finish the flower with very small petals in the center (Figure 20).

THE DAFFODIL
tip #104
2-inch waxed paper squares
yellow stamens

Daffodils can be made with the petals white and the centers yellow, or all yellow, with a stripe of orange added to enhance the outer edges of the petals and center cup. Attach the waxed paper square to the nail with a dab of icing. Pipe six petals around the center of the nail. These petals are made the same as the daisy. After the icing has set for several seconds, pinch the ends of the petals with your fingers to make a point (Figure 21).

To pipe the center of the flower, hold the tip so that the opening is perpendicular to the flower, with the wide end facing down. Place the tip in the center of the flower and pipe a cup as you turn the nail, ending the cup at the same point that you began. Insert three yellow stamens into the center of each flower (Figure 22).

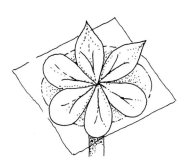

Figure 21

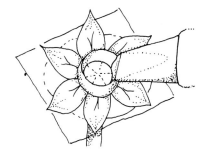

Figure 22

Flowers Made on the Lily Nail

THE LILY
tip #70
3-inch foil squares
stamens

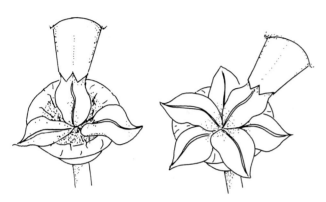

Figure 23   Figure 24

Press a foil square into the lily nail. Pipe three tip #70 petals out from the center of the nail (Figure 23). Pipe three more petals in between the first three petals (Figure 24). While the icing is wet, insert three or four stamens into the center of the flower. Carefully remove the foil from the nail without disturbing the flower. Allow two days to dry.

You can vary the type of lily by piping the petals more slowly, which will give the flower slightly rippled petals (Figure 25).

Figure 25

THE POINSETTIA AND DELPHINIUM
tips #66, #68
3-inch foil squares
stamens

Poinsettias and delphiniums are made the same way; the only difference is in the coloring. Poinsettias are usually all red or white, with yellow or green stamens, and delphiniums are usually blue for the outer petals and white or light blue for the inner petals, with blue or white stamens.

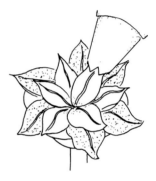

Figure 26

The base of these flowers is made the same way as the lily, using a smaller tip. After the first six petals are piped, six smaller petals are piped inside the outer six (Figure 26). Add five stamens to the centers.

THE PETUNIA
tip #103 or #104
3-inch foil squares
stamens

Fill a pastry bag with royal icing and attach the #103 tip. Press a foil square into the lily nail and fold the edges over and down. Place the wide end of the tip deep into the center of the nail. Start piping a petal similar to the way that the daisy petal is made, out from the center, to the edge of the nail, and then back to the center point. As you pipe the petal, shake the tip up and down to give the edge a rippled

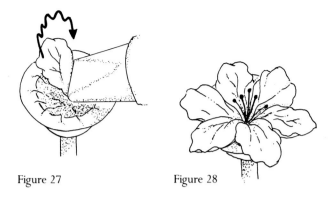

Figure 27   Figure 28

effect (Figure 27). Pipe six petals and insert five stamens (Figure 28). Allow to dry for two days.

Wired Flowers

Some flowers are piped on cloth-covered wires. Wires come in green, brown, and white. Green wires are the most natural, but if you are making a cake that is all white, use the white wires. After the flowers are completed and dried, wrap the wires with florist tape.

BABY'S BREATH
tip #14
3-inch lengths of green cloth-covered wire
green florist tape

Take six lengths of wire and twist them together, leaving about 1 inch at the top of each wire free. Fan out the six wires so that the ic-

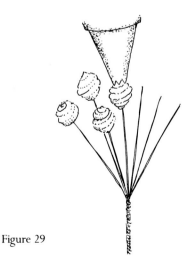

Figure 29

ing on each wire will not touch. With the #14 tip, pipe a white royal icing puff on the end of each wire (Figure 29).

THE HYACINTH AND HEATHER
tips #13, #19
4-inch lengths of green cloth-covered wire
green florist tape

A hyacinth can be made in any color, from deep purple and deep red to yellow and white. Fill a pastry bag with royal icing. Attach a #19 tip to the bag. Insert a wire about 2 inches through the tip and into the bag. Apply pres-

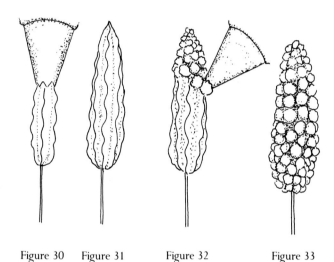

Figure 30   Figure 31   Figure 32   Figure 33

sure to the bag and slowly pull the wire out of the tip (Figure 30). The wire will be covered with rippled icing (Figure 31). Insert the stem of the flower into a piece of Styrofoam and allow to dry for twenty-four hours.

To make heather, the first step is the same as in making a hyacinth, except that the icing will be green (Figures 30 and 31).

Fill another pastry bag with lavender-colored icing and attach the #13 tip. Pipe puffs of lavender between the ridges of the green icing (Figure 32). Cover the entire flower (Figure 33). Place the stem into a piece of Styrofoam to dry for twenty-four hours.

Stemmed Flowers and Leaves

Icing flowers and leaves often need stems, particularly when they are to be placed into a sugar mold. Stems are made from round toothpicks for flowers and cloth-covered wires for leaves. Flat toothpicks are not strong enough to support flowers.

Cloth-covered wires come in green, but toothpicks need to be tinted, unless your cake is all white — then the toothpicks are left uncolored. Place a few drops of green liquid food coloring in a flat-bottomed bowl. Place the toothpicks in the bowl and mix until the toothpicks are coated with green dye. Remove the toothpicks and place on a double thickness of paper toweling. Allow the toothpicks to dry for a few hours.

Leaves are usually piped onto wires, since a wire can be cut to different lengths. Leaves usually extend farther out from a bouquet than do flowers. But leaves can also be made on toothpicks.

To attach dry icing flowers to stems, remove the waxed paper or foil on which the flower was piped. Turn the flower upside down on a

Figure 1

flat surface. Pipe a cone with the #7 tip and stiff green royal icing in the center of the back of the flower. Insert a toothpick into the cone (Figure 1). Let dry in this position for twenty-four hours.

To make leaves on wires, place a sheet of waxed paper on a cookie sheet. Cut green wires to 4-inch lengths. Tint stiff royal icing green by using either moss green paste coloring or leaf green with a little pink added. Fit a #5 tip onto a pastry bag and fill the bag with the green icing. Insert the wire about 2 inches into the tip. Apply pressure to the bag as you slowly pull the wire out. This will coat the wire with icing, making it easier for the leaf to adhere to

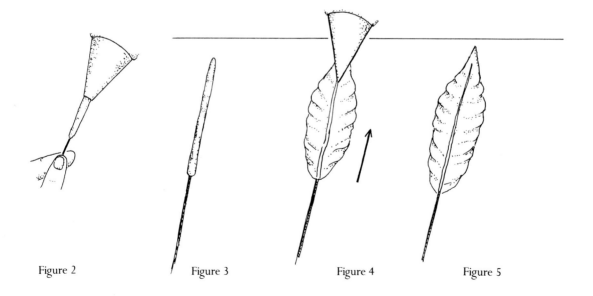

Figure 2

Figure 3

Figure 4

Figure 5

the wire (Figure 2). Place the wire on the waxed paper (Figure 3). Cover all of the wires needed.

When you have finished covering all of the wires, fit a #352 tip onto the pastry bag containing the green icing. I prefer to use this tip because the leaves always come to a point. Other leaf tips can be used, but unless the icing is soft, the leaf will end with a notch. Place the end of the tip with the point facing down on top of the icing-coated wire and pipe out toward the end (Figure 4). Allow the leaf to extend about ½ inch beyond the end of the wire (Figure 5). (Hint: Cover the wires with florist tape if they are to be inserted into the cake!) Let dry for twenty-four hours.

Bows in Royal Icing

Bows and ribbons can be a beautiful and festive addition to almost any cake. You can use practically any tip to make the loops for a bow, but the tips listed will start you out with the basic technique. Experiment with a number of different tips.

tips #48, #61, #103 or #104
waxed paper

Fit a tip onto a pastry bag. Place a sheet of waxed paper on a flat surface. Hold the end of the tip perpendicular to the paper. (If using a #61 or #103 tip, the wide end should be facing down.) Pipe a loop of icing onto the paper, making sure that each loop ends with a point (Figure 1). Make about thirty loops. Let dry for at least eight hours.

To construct the bow, squeeze out a mound of stiff royal icing the same color as the bow onto the surface of the cake, or onto a piece of waxed paper, if the bow is to be applied later. Begin placing the pointed tips of the dried loops into the mound in a circle around the base of the bow (Figure 2). Then add another circle of

loops inside the first layer, inserting the tips into the mound of icing. Add more icing to the center if necessary. Continue adding loops until a completed bow is formed (Figure 3). Allow to dry for twenty-four hours. To release the bow from the waxed paper, carefully slide a metal spatula under the bow and carefully set on the cake with a dab of icing to hold it in place.

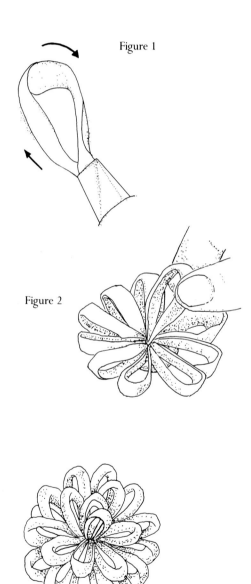

Figure 1

Figure 2

Figure 3

5

Gum Paste Decorations

Gum Paste Ribbons and Bows

There are two different types of bows made of gum paste. The first type is a knotted bow, while the second type is a pom-pom bow. The pom-pom loops and ribbons are made on toothpicks, then inserted into the cake.

    1 recipe gum paste
    plastic or marble cutting board
    small plastic or wooden rolling pin
    1 egg white, slightly beaten
    round toothpicks
    small dish of vegetable shortening
    small dish of dry gum paste mix

Cover a flat surface with nontextured paper towels or Kleenex. This creates a surface on which your ribbons can dry without sticking.

To make a knotted bow, tint the gum paste to the desired color and knead thoroughly. Rub a thin coating of vegetable shortening on a plastic or marble board. Roll the gum paste as thin as possible, lifting and turning the paste after every roll. Do not turn the paste over. Cut a strip about 8 inches long and 1½ inches wide. (This will make an average-sized bow. Vary the size of the bow by varying the size of the strip.) Take two pieces of Kleenex and roll them into

two tubes. Place them on the strip of gum paste, midway between the two halves of the strip (Figure 1). Dampen each end of the strip with a little water and lift up each end and place it in the center of the strip, pressing it into the center to stick to the bottom piece (Figure 2). The Kleenex will keep the gum paste from collapsing before it dries. Gently squeeze the center of the bow (Figure 3). Place the bow on a paper towel to dry.

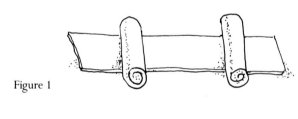
Figure 1

Figure 2

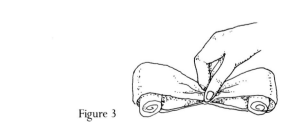
Figure 3

After the bow has set for about ten hours, you can add your center knot. Cut a strip of gum paste 1½ inches wide and about 2 inches long. Wrap the strip around the center of the bow and cut off any excess (Figure 4). Place the bow with the seam side down onto a piece of paper toweling and let the bow dry for at least twenty-four more hours.

To make the ribbon ends for the knotted bow, roll out some gum paste and cut a strip about 1½ inches wide by 6 inches long. Notch each end of the strip (Figure 5). Pinch together the center of the strip. Lay the strip on a piece of paper toweling, in a rippled formation, propping the ripples with pieces of Kleenex to hold their shape (Figure 6). Let the ribbon dry for two days.

To put together the knotted bow on your cake, place the ribbon ends in a mound of icing on the cake. Place the bow on more icing in the center of the ribbons (Figure 7).

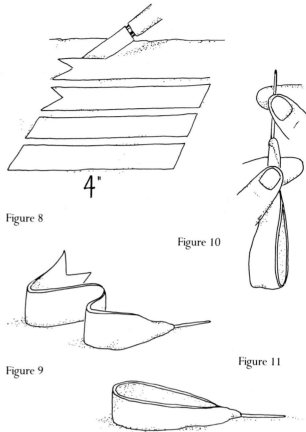

4"

Figure 8

Figure 9

Figure 10

Figure 11

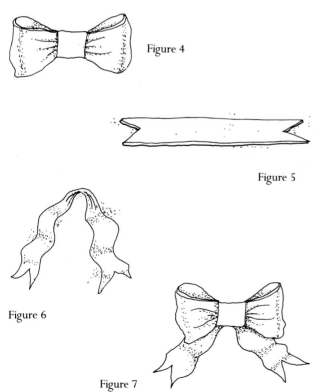

Figure 4

Figure 5

Figure 6

Figure 7

To make the ribbons for a pom-pom bow, cut 4-inch strips of gum paste with a sharp knife to the desired width and notch one end (Figure 8). Dip one end of a toothpick in the egg white and shake off the excess so that the toothpick is lightly coated. Wrap the unnotched end of the ribbon around the egg white end of the toothpick. Lay the strips out on the paper-covered board in a curved configuration (Figure 9).

To form loops, roll out the paste and cut to the same width as the ribbons. Cut the strip about 4 inches long. Dip a toothpick in the egg white and fold both ends around it (Figure 10). This will form a loop. Set the loop on its side on the paper-covered surface and let it dry (Figure 11). Allow them to dry for at least two days before placing them on your cake.

Have the dry gum paste mix handy while you are working and add small amounts to the paste if it starts to get sticky.

After every two or three times that you roll out the paste on the board, coat the board with more shortening to keep the paste from sticking.

Quick Rose

A fast and easy way to make a flower is to roll out a piece of gum paste and cut a strip about 1 inch wide by 3 inches long (Figure 12). Start rolling the paste until the size of the flower desired is reached (Figure 13). Using your finger tips, squeeze one end of the roll together and fan out the other end, to form a rose (Figure 14). You can also mix equal amounts of gum paste and rolled fondant to achieve the same results. Allow these flowers to dry for twenty-four hours.

Figure 12

Figure 13

Figure 14

6

Constructing Your Cake

Cake Boards

When creating a cake, keep in mind that the cake will need some kind of support. A crystal or silver platter, if you have one available, can enhance an elegant cake, but may not be appropriate for other types of cakes. Presentation is important, and the choice of the platter or board can either add to or detract from your labors.

I have found that a base made from foam board can be quite versatile and the board can be made to fit the shape and design of the cake. By using foam board, you can easily cut an odd shape that could not be found otherwise. You can also cover the board with thinned royal icing or colored foil, which can contrast with or complement the cake.

When using foam board as a base, you need to make sure that the board is thick enough to carry the weight of the cake. If the board is not thick enough, it will bend when you lift it and the cake will crack. I have found that corrugated cardboard is not strong enough, because it tends to bend no matter how many layers thick it is. Usually two layers of ¼-inch foam board glued together will be strong enough to hold a single or two-tiered cake. The wider the base of the cake is, the thicker the board should be.

Glue the boards with white glue and place some heavy books on top so that they dry flat.

To make a base from foam board, trace the outline of the shape that you want on the board and cut it out with a sharp X-acto knife. The board should be at least 2 inches wider on all sides than the cake.

A simple way to cover the board is to use foil wrap that is specifically made for cake decorating. Foil wrap comes in a variety of colors and patterns and can be purchased at cake-decorating stores. Place the foam board on the foil and cut out a piece that overlaps each side of the board by 2 inches. Wrap the foil around the board and tape to the bottom with masking tape.

To cover a board with icing to match the cake, glue the boards together to the desired thickness. Let the glue dry completely. Take enough royal icing to cover the board, and thin with water until the icing is the consistency of syrup. Tint the icing, if desired, and pour onto the board. Smooth with a spatula and set aside to dry for twenty-four hours.

Since this method leaves the edge of the board uncovered, a ribbon or a border of royal icing is placed around the edge of the board. To place a ribbon on the edge of the board, put a thin layer of glue around the edge and wrap the appropriate thickness of ribbon all around. This gives the cake a very elegant and professional look.

To make a piped border of royal icing around the board, place the board on a piece of waxed paper that extends out from all sides of the board. Pipe a border of royal icing around the bare edge of the board, using a tip large enough to cover the edge. Let it dry for twenty-four hours. This method makes it difficult to carry the cake without cracking the icing, so a smaller board should be glued underneath the icing-covered board after the border has dried. (Remove the waxed paper before gluing on the smaller board.) This will enable you to pick up the board easily.

When using a board covered with royal icing, you must place the bottom tier of the cake on a separator board. After the cake is iced, it is then placed on the bottom board with a dab of icing to hold it in place.

Whenever a cake is set on any kind of plate or board, a dab of icing is used to "glue" the cake in place. This prevents the cake from shifting. A dab of icing is also used to "glue" multiple tiers together. About a tablespoon of buttercream is enough to keep the cake in place.

Servings

For serving most cakes, the following table lists how many servings you can expect from various sized and shaped cake pans and the number of cake recipes you will need for each. Most cake recipes yield approximately 6 cups of batter, which serves about twenty people. Each pan should be filled with batter halfway to insure maximum baking efficiency. Serving sizes vary, depending on who is cutting the cake, but the amounts given measure about 3–4 inches high and 1x2 inches wide.

Pan Size	Servings	Number of Cake Recipes
6-inch round	10	½
7-inch round	15	¾
8-inch round	20	1
9-inch round	25	1
10-inch round	35	1½
12-inch round	50	2
14-inch round	70	3
15-inch round	85	3½
16-inch round	100	4
6-inch square	15	¾
8-inch square	30	1
9-inch square	40	1½
10-inch square	50	2
12-inch square	70	3
14-inch square	100	4
16-inch square	125	5
6-inch ball	10	1
9x13-inch rectangle	20	1
11x15-inch rectangle	35	1½
12-inch heart	25	2

Assembly of Tiered Cakes

A layer is the amount of cake baked in one pan. The cakes in this book are generally made by placing one layer on top of another with filling in between. A tiered cake is made up of graduated layers. When making a cake with more than one tier, you have to reinforce the structure so that the weight of the layers does not make the bottom of the cake collapse. The structure is only as strong as its foundation. The additional support is provided by ¼-inch-wide wooden dowels or plastic drinking straws inserted into the cake. Each tier is set on a board, which supports the cake on top of the dowels.

Each separator board (the board between the tiers) should have the same circumference as the cake that it is supporting. Pre-cut corrugated boards can be purchased in cake-decorating supply stores, but I prefer foam board because it is lightweight yet sturdy. You can find foam board in most art supply stores and it can be easily and cleanly cut with an X-acto knife.

To make separator boards for each tier, place the bottom of the pan in which your cake was baked on a piece of foam board. Draw an outline around the pan and cut out the shape. This will give you a board the exact size as your tier.

After you have baked your cakes, they will usually not be perfectly flat on the top. Cut off the tops of the cakes with a serrated knife to make the cakes level. It is easier to cut a cake that has been wrapped in plastic or foil and refrigerated for a few hours; there is less crumbling.

Place the cake on the board with a dab of icing so that the top of the cake is facing down. This will give you a smooth and even surface. Fill in any gaps around the base of the cake with icing. Add filling to the top of the bottom layer and then place the second layer on top of the first one, top side down. Fill in any gaps between the layers with icing.

To construct a 3-tiered cake that has tiers 12 inches, 8 inches, and 6 inches wide, each tier being two layers thick, place the bottom layer of each cake on its corresponding separator board, using a dab of icing spread on the board to hold the cake in place. Spread filling on the bottom layer and then set the top layer on top of the filling. Ice the top and sides of the tier.

Place the 12-inch tier onto a cake plate or prepared board, using a dab of icing to keep it in place. When the icing on the top of the 12-inch tier is dry to the touch, place the bottom of the 8-inch pan on the center of the 12-inch tier. Lightly outline the pan with a toothpick. This will give you a perimeter in which to insert your dowels. Insert a dowel into the center of the 12-inch tier until it touches the board.

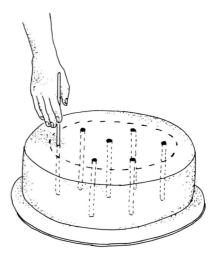

Figure 1

Cut off the dowel slightly below the top of the cake. Insert six more dowels around the inside of the 8-inch circle and cut off the excess (Figure 1).

Plastic drinking straws can also be used as supports and are much easier to cut, but they are not strong enough to support very large or heavy tiers.

Spread a thin layer of icing on the top of the 12-inch tier to cover the dowels. Then place the 8-inch tier on its separator board on top of the 12-inch tier. Outline the 6-inch pan on top of the 8-inch cake and insert dowels as you did on the 12-inch tier (Figure 2).

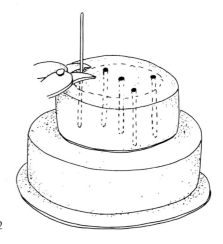

Figure 2

The top tier does not need any supports, unless you are placing a heavy decoration on the top of the cake. In that case, you can insert a single dowel in the top of the 6-inch tier to support your decoration.

If the bottom tier is larger than 12 inches, insert eight or nine dowels to give it added support.

When using columns, pre-made plastic separator plates are used instead of foam boards. These plates have pegs on which the columns are placed. To support the plates, dowels are used in the same manner as above, except that these plates have indentations on the bottom to show you where to place the dowels. Press the plate gently into the dry icing on top of the tier on which it will be sitting and carefully lift off. Insert your dowels into the impressions left by the bottom of the plate (Figure 3). When delivering a tiered cake, keep the tiers in separate

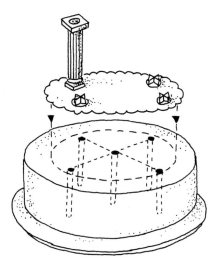

Figure 3

boxes until you arrive at your destination. Otherwise, your cake may collapse. Set up your cake when you arrive, making sure you bring extra icing for last-minute borders or touch-ups.

Part

II

───⦅≈≈≈⦆───

Beginner
Cakes

Scallop Shell Cake

The scallop shell cake is baked in a shell-shaped pan and is decorated using a toothpick, a paintbrush, and a little food coloring. It's perfect for a summertime beach party.

Serves 20

12-inch shell-shaped cake
1 recipe rolled fondant
1 recipe buttercream icing
#1 and #4 round paintbrushes
round toothpicks
brown and copper paste food coloring
unsweetened cocoa powder
16-inch platter
1 cup sugar
1 tablespoon brown sugar

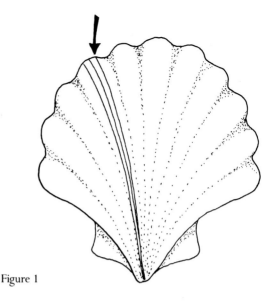

Figure 1

In advance:

Make the fondant and let it set overnight at room temperature, wrapped in plastic and placed in an airtight container.

To decorate the cake:

Bake the cake and let it cool completely. Set the cake on a 16-inch platter with a dab of buttercream to hold it in place. Cover the cake with a thin layer of buttercream. Roll out the fondant and place on the cake, smoothing the fondant with your hands.

Using the handle end of a large paintbrush, gently run along the indented lines of the shell. Start at the wide end of the shell and work toward the front of the cake. This will deepen the lines of the shell.

Take a toothpick and indent lines along the ridges of the shell, pulling the toothpick toward you. Make three lines along each ridge (Figure 1).

With the tip of a sharp steak knife, make small horizontal lines along the length of each indented line (Figure 2).

Dip the larger paintbrush into some cocoa powder and generously dust the surface of the

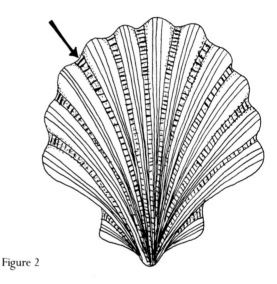

Figure 2

cake with cocoa. Clean off the brush and brush off the excess cocoa.

Mix a little copper food coloring with a few drops of water in a small bowl. Dip the larger paintbrush in the coloring and paint five curved horizontal lines across the surface of the cake, following the curve of the shell. Feather the painted lines with the small paintbrush dipped in the thinned copper coloring (Figure 3).

Mix a little brown coloring with water and paint the back edge and two thin lines across the next two copper lines, using the small paintbrush. Feather the lines (Figure 4).

Thin the brown coloring with a few more drops of water and paint along the tops and bottoms of the top three horizontal copper lines. Feather the lines with the small brush (Figure 5).

To give the impression that the cake is surrounded by sand, mix about 1 tablespoon brown sugar with 1 cup of white sugar and sprinkle around the base of the cake.

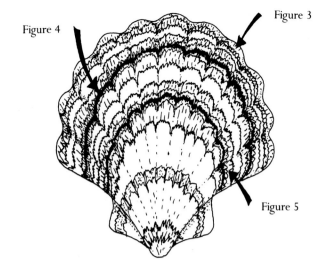

Figure 4

Figure 3

Figure 5

Joanne's Birthday Cake

This cake was inspired by the expressionistic roses my friend Joanne Suzuki paints on her pottery, shown in the photograph. It's a fun and easy cake to make and you don't have to worry about being a perfectionist.

Serves 20

8-inch round cake, 4 inches high (2 layers)
2 12-inch scalloped-edged cake boards (found in cake-decorating stores) glued together, or a 12-inch round cake stand
1 recipe rolled fondant
1 recipe buttercream icing
1 recipe royal icing
purple, blue, pink, and green paste colors
⅜-inch-wide pink ribbon
tips #2, #352

In advance:

Make the rolled fondant and wrap it in plastic. Let it set overnight at room temperature.

To decorate the cake:

Bake cake layers and allow them to cool. Secure the bottom layer to the board or plate with a dab of buttercream in the center, add filling, then add the top layer. Cover the cake with buttercream.

Break off a piece of the fondant about 2 inches wide. Knead some pink and a tiny bit of purple paste coloring into the fondant. Knead until the colors are only slightly mixed. Set aside wrapped in plastic.

Tint the remaining fondant by adding small amounts of purple and blue coloring and kneading until the colors are slightly mixed, but not completely. This will give the fondant a marbled look.

Roll out the large piece of fondant to an 8-inch-diameter circle. Take the pink fondant and break off small pieces and flatten them with your hands. Make about twenty pieces of various sizes, ranging from ½ inch to 2 inches wide. Press the flat pink pieces onto the large piece of fondant. When all of the pink fondant pieces have been placed, continue rolling out the fondant to the correct size to fit over the cake. Lay the fondant on the cake. (If you are using the scalloped boards, roll the fondant so that it will cover the cake and the edge of the board.) Cut away the excess fondant from the bottom edge of the cake, or cut around the scalloped edge.

Wrap the pink ribbon around the bottom edge of the cake and glue the ends down with a tiny dab of buttercream icing.

Tint ¼ cup of the white royal icing a pale pink. Thin with a few drops of water. Using the #2 tip, make concentric rose petals using a thick and thin manner. Start squeezing the pastry bag lightly to start and then increase pressure for the middle of the petal; then let the icing trail to a point. Make large and small roses all over the cake in the pink areas.

Tint another ¼ cup of royal icing a darker pink and pipe #2 thin lines in between the

thicker light pink lines. Pipe tiny rose outlines in a spiral around the surface of the cake (Figure 1).

Tint about ½ cup of the royal icing a dark green. Pipe green stems with the #2 tip between the pink areas. Add small green leaves with the #352 tip so that they are raised off the surface of the cake. Add small green dots all around with the #2 tip.

Figure 1

Dessert Cactus Cake

Believe it or not, everything is edible on this cake, including the needles and the cookie crumb "dirt." The cactus makes an interesting centerpiece for a housewarming party.

Serves 10

6-inch ball cake
1 recipe royal icing
large lily nail
aluminum foil
small yellow stamens
waxed paper
1 recipe basic buttercream icing
20 chocolate wafer cookies, crushed (place the cookies in a plastic bag and roll with a rolling pin)
3 inch high by 7½ inch wide clean clay flowerpot
green, lemon yellow, and pink paste colors
tips #2, #32, #68

In advance:

Make the cactus flower: Tint ½ cup of stiff royal icing a bright pink. Using the large lily nail lined with aluminum foil and the #68 leaf tip, pipe petals all around the nail (Figure 1). Make a second row of petals inside the first row of petals (Figure 2). While the icing is still wet, insert about 50 yellow stamens into the center of the flower (Figure 3). Set the flower aside to dry for two days.

Next, make about 300 needles. Tint ¼ cup of royal icing pale yellow and with the #2 tip pipe ½-inch lines on a sheet of waxed paper. Let these dry for a few hours.

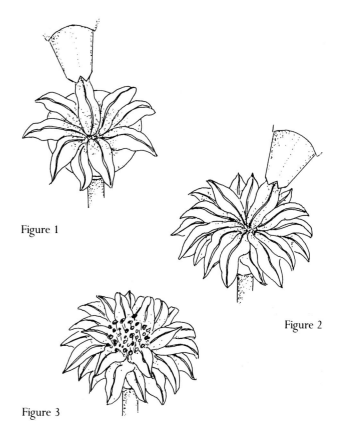

Figure 1

Figure 2

Figure 3

To decorate the cake:

Bake the cake in two halves of the 6-inch ball pan and cool.

Line the clay pot with aluminum foil. Take half of the crushed cookies and place them in the clay pot. Place one of the half ball cakes, flat side up, on top of the cookie crumbs. Place filling on the cake and then add the top half of the cake. Make green buttercream icing for the cactus by mixing green food coloring with a little pink to get the dusty green of a cactus.

Cover the cake with a thin layer of the green buttercream icing. Add the remaining cookie crumbs around the base of the cake to keep it in place.

Fit a pastry bag with a #32 star tip and fill with the green icing. Pipe stars in a line, working from the bottom to the top of the ball. Use less pressure on the bag as you approach the top, so that the stars are a little smaller as you work up. Insert five needles into the center of each star while the icing is still wet (Figure 4). Continue around the entire ball until it is completely covered with stars and needles. Leave part of the top without needles so there is room for the cactus flower. Place the dried flower into the wet buttercream.

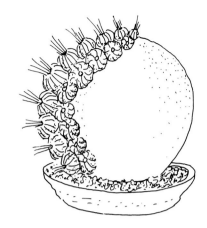

Figure 4

Christmas Wreath

Christmas wouldn't be Christmas without a wreath. This rustic looking grapevine wreath looks real enough to hang on the door, and looks just as good on the dessert table.

Serves 15

10-inch ring cake
1 recipe royal icing
waxed paper
1 recipe stiff chocolate buttercream icing (add ¼ cup unsweetened cocoa to the basic buttercream recipe)
large silver dragees
Boston Baked Bean candies
cloth-covered wires
brown florist tape
red paste food coloring
tips #1D, #104, #363

In advance:

Make the bow and ribbons on waxed paper with the red royal icing and the #104 tip (see page 21). Pipe two large loops about 3 inches long. Pipe two 3-inch ribbons by zigzagging the icing as it comes out of the tip. Make a few extra in case of breakage. Set aside to dry for eight hours.

To decorate the cake:

Bake the cake and allow to cool. Place the cake on a cake plate. Cover the cake with thinned chocolate icing. Start piping the vines with the stiff chocolate icing and the #363 tip. Start piping from the inside of the wreath, over

the top of the cake and down the side. Continue piping overlapping lines of icing and cover the entire cake.

When the surface is covered, pipe six diagonal ribbons from inside of the wreath to the outside with the red royal icing and the #1D tip. Make sure to leave a space at the bottom for the bow.

To form the bow, pipe a mound of red royal icing onto the top of the cake in the space reserved for the bow. Set the two ribbons in the icing. Pipe another mound of icing in the center of the ribbons and insert the loops. Finish the bow with a short line of icing using the #104 tip to "tie" the bow together (Figure 1).

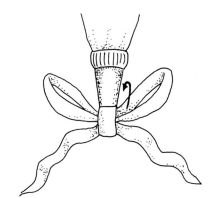

Figure 1

Add the dragees and the Boston Baked Bean candies by piping small dots of chocolate icing and placing the candies into the wet icing.

Twist together two 6-inch lengths of wire. Make six of these doubled wires. Wrap the

wires with brown florist tape. Twist the doubled wire around a pencil to form a tight coil.
Remove from the pencil and gently pull on the
wire to elongate it. Insert the wires into the
cake to give the look of a grapevine.

Fish Cake

I designed this cake for some friends of mine who were moving to Seattle. It looked so real that everyone wondered where the dessert was!

All of the decorating on the fish is done by embossing the rolled fondant.

Serves 15

9x13-inch rectangle cake
18-inch oval platter
1 recipe rolled fondant
1 recipe buttercream icing
silver and iridescent white edible powders
lemon extract
small paintbrush
candied lemon slices
1 black licorice button candy, ¼ inch wide
corn syrup
blue, green, and red food coloring
tips #4, #65, #103, #104

In advance:

Make the rolled fondant and let set overnight at room temperature.

To decorate the cake:

Bake the cake and allow to cool. Cut the cake as illustrated (Figure 1). Reserve the excess cake. Round off the cut edges. Place the cake on a large platter with a dab of buttercream to hold it in place. Cut a triangular piece of cake from the remaining cake (using the tail drawing — Figure 7 on page 45 — as a guide) and attach to the back of the fish with a little icing. Trim the top surface of the tail so that it is not as high as the body of the fish.

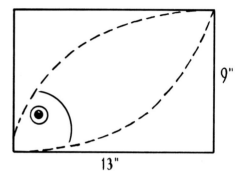

Figure 1

Cover the entire fish with a thin layer of buttercream icing and then cover the body with rolled fondant. Using a toothpick, mark the gill area by gently pressing into the fondant. To make the scales, take a thin decorating tip, such as a #4, and, using the back of the tip, press it into the cake at an angle, to the right of the gills, so that you get a half-circle impression (Figure 2). Make a succession of scales along the

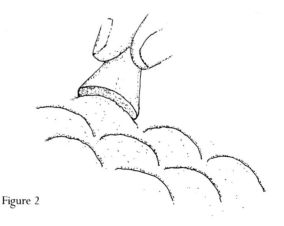

Figure 2

gill line. For the next line of scales, make the half circles in between the first scales. Continue making scales over the entire body.

To make the fins, roll out the remaining fondant to a thickness of about ¼ inch. Trace and cut out the patterns for the fins (Figures 3, 4, 5, and 6). Take a toothpick and score the fins with many lines by dragging the toothpick along the fondant. Let the toothpick break the fondant at the end to give the fins a ragged look. With a small paintbrush, brush a little water onto the body of the fish where the fins will be attached. Press the fins in place. Slightly ruffle the fins after they have been attached.

To make the tail, cut out the fondant, using the pattern for the tail (Figure 7). Score in the same manner as the fins. Dampen the end of the cake and place the fondant tail on the cake. This piece should extend out past the cake.

To make the lips, roll a thin piece of fondant into a rope about ¼ inch thick. Brush the lip area of the fish's head with a little water and attach an upper and lower lip.

To color the fish, add ¼ teaspoon white iri-

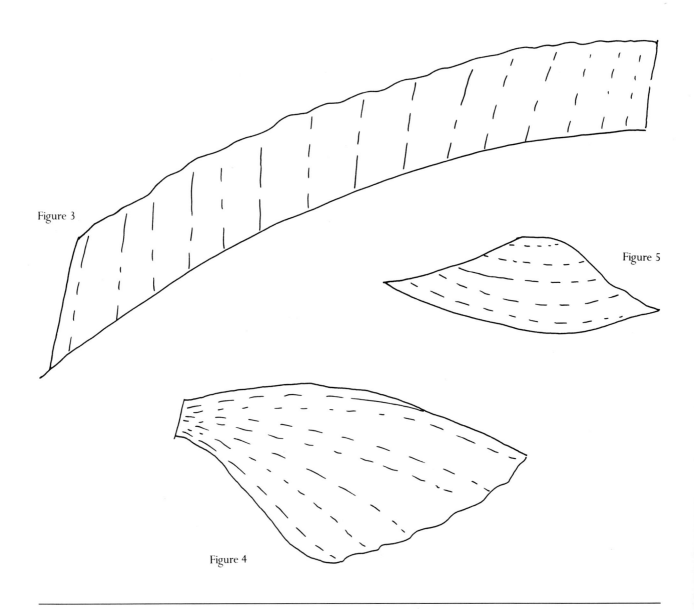

Figure 3

Figure 5

Figure 4

descent powder to a few drops of lemon extract until you have a thin paint consistency. Paint the bottom half of the fish white. Next, add silver powder to some lemon extract and paint the rest of the fish silver, including the head. Thin some royal blue paste color with water and paint a horizontal stripe across the middle of the fish. Paint blue vertical stripes from the middle strip up to the top of the fish. Paint the ends of the fins and tail with the blue color.

Pipe a white circle of buttercream on the eye area and press the licorice candy into the icing.

To garnish the platter, first make the cherry tomatoes. Tint the remaining fondant red and roll into 1¼-inch balls. To make the tomatoes shiny, brush with a little corn syrup. Tint the remaining buttercream green and pipe small leaves on top of the tomatoes with the #65 tip. Fit a #104 tip onto the pastry bag and pipe the greens all around the platter. You can vary the size of the leaves with the #103 tip. Place the cherry tomatoes and candied lemon slices in the green buttercream around the fish.

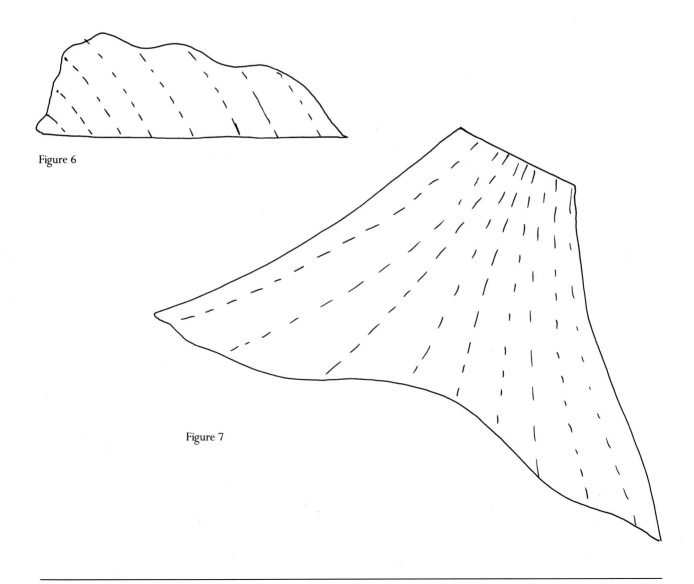

Figure 6

Figure 7

Halloween Witch's Hat

The run-in sugar bats appear to be flying around the moon above the witch's hat. It will be a perfect surprise for the kids when they return from trick-or-treating.

Serves 20

Cakes:

8-inch round, 3 inches high (2 layers)
6-inch round, 3 inches high (2 layers)
1 recipe royal icing
waxed paper
7 cloth-covered wires, 8 inches long
1 tablespoon vodka
brown florist tape
black and yellow edible glitter
12-inch round foam board, 2 layers thick
icing comb
8-inch round foam board
plastic drinking straw
1 recipe chocolate buttercream icing (add ¼ cup unsweetened cocoa to the basic buttercream recipe)
Styrofoam cone, 4 inches high and 3 inches wide at the base
candy corn
large and small silver dragees
black and orange paste food coloring
tips #3, #7, #22

In advance:

Tint the wires black by mixing a little black paste coloring with the vodka and placing it in a flat-bottomed bowl. Add the wires and mix until the wires are coated with the coloring. Place the wires on a paper towel to dry.

Figure 1

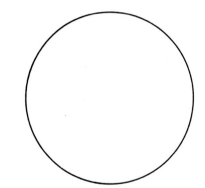

Figure 2

Make the run-in sugar bats and moon using the patterns provided (Figures 1 and 2). Tint about ½ cup of royal icing black. Trace the patterns for the bats and moon on a sheet of paper. Place the bat pattern under a piece of waxed paper. Place the moon pattern under another piece of waxed paper. Outline the bats with stiff black royal icing, using the #3 tip. Set a black wire in the center of the design. Make six bats. When the bats have all been outlined, thin the remaining black icing with some water to make it runny (see the section on run-in sugar on page 8) and fill in the bats with the #3 tip. Sprinkle the bats with

black edible glitter after each one has been made.

Tint a small amount of royal icing orange and outline the moon, with a wire set into the design. Fill in with orange run-in sugar and sprinkle with yellow glitter. Set the designs aside to dry for a day. When all of the designs have dried, carefully turn each one over and repeat the same procedure on the reverse side. Add two small dragees to the bats for the eyes. Sprinkle with glitter and let dry. When dry, wrap all of the ends of the wires with brown florist tape.

To prepare the 12-inch board, tint about one cup royal icing black. Do not thin the icing. Tape the bottom of the board onto a piece of waxed paper that is larger than the board. Tape the waxed paper and the board onto a turntable. Cover the board with black royal icing and comb the icing with the icing comb, while turning the turntable (Figure 3). Sprinkle black glitter on the wet icing. Shake off the excess glitter. Pipe beads of black icing with the #7 tip around the edge of the board and place large silver dragees into the icing all around the

border. Set this aside to dry for twenty-four hours.

To decorate the cake:

Bake the cakes and allow them to cool. (Hint: Freezing the cakes for a few hours in advance makes them easier to carve.) Stack the cakes on an 8-inch round foam core board, placing filling in between the layers. Insert a plastic straw into the center of the cake all the way to the board. This will keep the cake steady.

Place the Styrofoam cone on a piece of waxed paper the same diameter as the bottom of the cone. Attach the cone to the waxed paper with a dab of buttercream. Place the cone on the top of the cake in the center. Carve the cakes with a serrated knife to form the cone (Figure 4). Remove the Styrofoam cone from

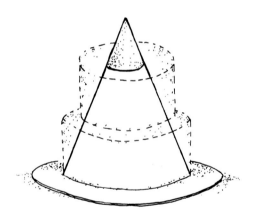

Figure 4

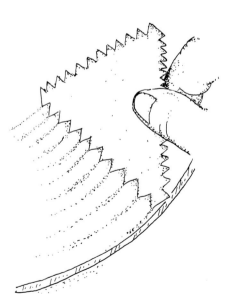

Figure 3

the top of the cake. Coat the cake with thinned chocolate buttercream. Secure the cake to the prepared board with a dab of buttercream.

Insert the wired bats and moon into the Styrofoam cone. Push the ends of the wires through the bottom of the cone and through the waxed paper so they extend about ½ inch from the bottom of the cone. Place the cone on top of the cake with a dab of buttercream, pushing the wires into the top of the cake.

Cover the cake with chocolate icing piped from the #22 tip. Start at the bottom of the cake and pipe zigzag lines up the cake to the top. The icing lines should fill in the surface of the cake. The zigzags should be about 1½ inches wide at the bottom and taper off as you go up until the icing becomes just a thin line (Figure 5). Sprinkle each zigzag of icing with black glitter as you go, so that the glitter adheres to the wet icing. Gently brush off the excess glitter around the base with a soft brush when finished.

Pipe dots of icing around the base of the cake and add a line of candy corn to form the hat band, using the photograph as a guide.

Figure 5

Popcorn Bowl

This is a great cake to make for an April Fool's Day surprise or for a sweet distraction at a Super Bowl party.

Serves 25

1 cake baked in a 10-inch metal bowl (bake as you would in a normal cake pan)
1 recipe royal icing
waxed paper
9x12-inch foam board, 2 layers thick
2 recipes off-white basic buttercream icing
unsweetened cocoa powder
5¼-inch round foam board
blue, red, brown, and orange paste food coloring
tips #4, #7, #11, #18, #46, #48

One day in advance:

To make the board that the cake will sit on, place the rectangular board on a sheet of waxed paper, making sure that the paper is larger than the board. Secure the board to the paper with a dab of royal icing. Draw a line parallel to each of the short ends of the board 1 inch wide, which is the space for the fringed edge. Tint ½ cup of the royal icing a bright red. Pipe alternating white stripes (with the #48 tip) and red stripes (with the #46 tip) along the 9-inch length of the board, leaving 1 inch on the left and right end undecorated. Tint another ½ cup of the icing a bright blue. Pipe blue lines with the #18 tip equally spaced along the 12-inch length of the board, crossing the red and white stripes. Pipe alternating white and blue fringe in the 1-inch spaces on either end, using the #4 tip. Pipe a white loop border with the #4 tip

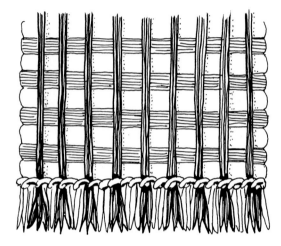

Figure 1

along the inside edge where the fringe meets the stripes (Figure 1). Set the board aside to dry for twenty-four hours.

To decorate the cake:

Bake the cake in the 10-inch metal bowl, greased and floured as you would with any other cake pan. (Hint: Reduce the oven temperature slightly so that the center of the cake bakes completely without burning the edges.) Cool slightly and remove the cake from the bowl. Cool completely.

You may first have to flatten the top of the cake slightly if it is rounded cutting with a serrated knife. (Turn the cake upside down onto a piece of waxed paper.) (Hint: Using a turntable makes decorating this cake much easier.) Cover the sides of the cake with thinned dark brown

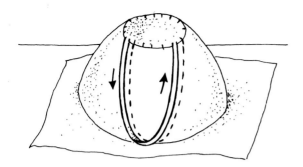

Figure 2

buttercream icing (add unsweetened cocoa powder to the basic buttercream). With the cake still upside down, divide the bottom (now on top) into sixteen equal sections and mark with a toothpick. (See the section on marking divisions on the cake on page 13.) Tint about 1½ cups of the buttercream with yellow food coloring and a little cocoa powder to make a straw color. With the #48 tip, pipe a loop of icing starting at one division, piping down the side of the cake, to the bottom of the cake and then up to the sixth division (Figure 2). The natural movement of the arm will automatically cause the icing to twist as you start to bring the icing back up to the top of the cake. (You can practice piping this movement on the outer edge of your metal bowl to gain some confidence before you start on the cake.) The next loop starts to the right of the first one, at the second division, and ends at the seventh division. Continue in this manner. When you reach the sixth division, start piping the next loop beside the icing from the end of the first loop. Cover the entire cake with loops. Let the icing set for about twenty minutes before turning the cake right side up.

Before turning the cake over, spread some icing on the upright center of the cake and place the round foam board on top of the icing. Place a dab of icing in the center of the prepared foam board rectangle. Slide your hand under the waxed paper that the cake is resting on and place the other hand on the round foam board. Turn the cake over and, being careful not to disturb the icing decoration, set the cake on the prepared board. Pipe a border of straw-colored icing around the base of the cake with the #18 tip.

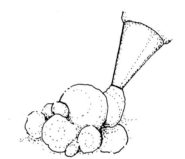

Figure 3

Next, cover the top of the cake with a thin layer of white buttercream. Pipe large round mounds of icing with the #11 tip and cover the surface of the cake. Next, switch to the #7 tip and pipe smaller mounds in between the large ones (Figure 3). Don't try to make the mounds uniform, as the popcorn will not look natural. To finish the cake, thin some brown food coloring with a little water and paint small dots of coloring in between some of the "kernels."

Father's Day Sweater

Why not give Dad a sweater for Father's Day? One that you made yourself. You don't even have to know how to knit. And even the box is edible.

Serves 20

9x13-inch sheet cake
9½x13½-inch foam board, 2 layers thick
1 recipe royal icing
waxed paper
1 recipe basic buttercream icing
unsweetened cocoa powder
ruler
blue, copper, and brown paste food coloring
tips #3, #16, #48

In advance:

Make the run-in sugar sides for the gift box. Draw four rectangles on a piece of paper, two measuring 13½ inches by 3¼ inches, and two measuring 9½ inches by 3¼ inches. Place a piece of waxed paper over each rectangle and tape down the sides. Outline the rectangles on the waxed paper with blue royal icing, using the #3 tip. Thin the royal icing with water as directed for run-in sugar (page 8) and fill in the rectangles with the thinned blue icing. Let the panels dry overnight.

When the rectangles have dried, pipe white royal icing stripes on each rectangle with the flat side of the #48 tip, leaving equal space between each stripe. Let the panels dry for twenty-four hours.

To decorate the cake:

Bake the cake and let it cool completely. Cut the top of the cake to form the neckline (Figure 1). Secure the cake to the foam board with a dab of buttercream. Ice the cake with thinned brown buttercream icing. (Add a little unsweetened cocoa to the basic buttercream icing.)

Mark off a grid of 1-inch squares with a toothpick on the surface of the cake. Mark the pattern of the sweater on the cake, using the illustration as a guide (Figure 2). Tint 1 cup of buttercream a beige color. Tint ½ cup each of buttercream blue, dark brown, and copper.

The entire sweater is piped in loops using the #3 tip (Figure 3). It's easier to decorate this cake if you have four #3 tips attached to four separate pastry bags, one bag for each color.

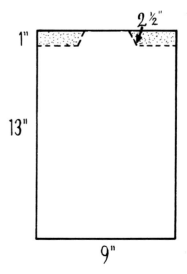

Figure 1

From the two of us, Dad.

Figure 3

Start at the top of the cake and pipe beige loops horizontally, down 3 inches. Pipe the neckline with the #16 tip and beige icing, using a zigzag motion (Figure 4).

To pipe the rest of the sweater, follow the color patterns in the photograph. When you come to an area that contains a triangle or a diamond shape, pipe the entire shape and then continue around it in the appropriate background color.

When you have finished piping the sweater, remove the striped run-in sugar panels from the waxed paper and set them against the sides of the board, piping a thick band of royal icing along the edge to hold the panels in place. Pipe some royal icing in the inside corners of the panels to give them extra strength. Let the icing dry overnight. Carefully place tissue paper inside the box around the sweater after the royal icing has set.

Figure 4

1"{

1"

Figure 2

Peach Chapeau

A pretty little tea cake for Mom, this is a cake she would love to receive on Mother's Day or any other day. The embossed rolled fondant makes it look elegant, yet it is very simple to do.

Serves 10

Cakes:

half of a 6-inch ball
6-inch round, 2 inches high

1 recipe rolled fondant
1 recipe royal icing
waxed paper
9-inch round foam board
1 recipe buttercream icing
small rose petal gum paste cutter
baby's breath gum paste cutter
toothpicks
11-inch cake stand
pink and yellow paste food coloring
tip #2

In advance:

Make the rolled fondant and tint it a pale peach color, using a little pink and yellow coloring. Set it aside overnight at room temperature, wrapped securely in plastic.

Next, to make the run-in sugar ornament for the front of the hat, draw a 2-inch circle on a piece of paper. Place a piece of waxed paper over the circle. On the waxed paper, outline the circle with peach-colored royal icing, using the #2 tip. Fill in the circle with thinned peach royal icing. Let this dry for two hours. Then,

Figure 1

pipe a ⅜-inch-wide dot in the center of the circle with the thinned peach icing, using the #2 tip. Cover the rest of the circle with small dots of royal icing (Figure 1). Let this dry for twenty-four hours.

To decorate the cake:

Bake the cakes and let them cool completely. Attach the 6-inch round cake to the foam board with a dab of icing so that the cake is off center on the board. The cake should be ½ inch from one edge of the circle and 2½ inches from the opposite edge. The board will make the brim of the hat (Figure 2). Place filling on the top of

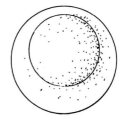

Figure 2

the 6-inch layer and place the 6-inch half ball on top. Cover the entire cake and the visible part of the board with buttercream. Place the cake and board on the cake stand, secured with a dab of buttercream.

Peach Chapeau, Peach Purse Cake, Fabergé Jewelry Box

Roll out the fondant to make a 14-inch circle that is ¼ inch thick. Carefully place the fondant over the top of the cake and over the board. Smooth the fondant and trim around the edge of the board, so that the fondant covers the edge.

Emboss a rose petal border with the cutter in the fondant around the edge of the hat brim. Press the baby's breath cutter into the center of each rose petal. With a toothpick, make dots between each petal on the outer edge of the circle. Make smaller toothpick dots all around the inner edge of the petals (Figure 3).

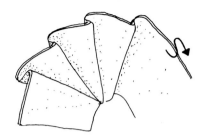

Figure 4

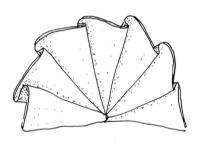

Figure 5

Figure 3

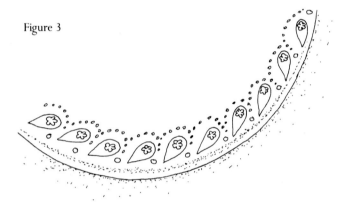

Measure the circumference of the base of the dome with a tape measure. Add pink coloring to the remaining fondant and knead until the color is completely blended. Roll out the fondant to a thickness of ⅛ inch. Cut a strip 1 inch wide and as long as the circumference of the base of the dome. Brush a little water around the bottom edge of the dome and wrap the fondant strip around the moistened area. Begin and end the strip in the back of the dome. Gently press the strip to the cake. Cut another strip of fondant that is the same length as the first strip, but ½ inch wide. Place this centered on the first strip in the same manner.

Roll out the remaining fondant to the same thickness and cut a strip 2½ inches wide and about 15 inches long. Start folding the strip in a fan shape (Figure 4). Keep folding until you have a semicircle, and cut off the excess fondant (Figure 5). Brush a little water on the front of the cake and carefully set the fondant fan in place.

To finish the cake, pipe a dot of buttercream to the back of the royal icing disk and place it in the center of the fan-shaped ornament.

Peach Purse Cake

The purse cake is a perfect accessory for the Peach Chapeau and is decorated in the same manner, by embossing the rolled fondant.

Serves 15

6-inch square cake, 2 inches high
1 recipe royal icing
waxed paper
gold edible powder
lemon extract
1 recipe rolled fondant
1 recipe buttercream icing
small flower-shaped gum paste cutters, ½ inch
    wide
toothpicks
10-inch silver platter or 10-inch round foam board
    covered with silver foil
pink and yellow food coloring
tips #2, #14

In advance:

Make the 2-inch run-in sugar disc in the same manner as described in the directions for the Peach Chapeau (page 56). When dry, paint the center dot with a little gold powder mixed with lemon extract (use about ⅛ teaspoon powder to a few drops of extract).

Make peach-colored rolled fondant with pink and yellow food coloring. Let it set, wrapped in plastic at room temperature for twenty-four hours.

To decorate the cake:

Bake the cake and cool. Cut off the top of the cake on an angle, starting at the top of the

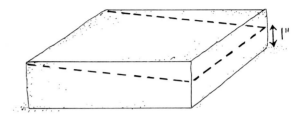

Figure 1

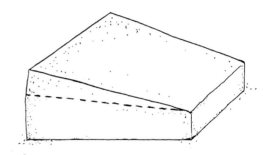

Figure 2

cake and cutting down 1 inch (Figure 1). Place the bottom section of the cake on the platter or board, using a dab of buttercream to hold it in place. Place filling on top of this layer. Place the cut portion of the cake on the reverse side of the bottom layer (Figure 2).

Cover the cake with a coat of thinned buttercream. Then, cover the cake with peach fondant. Roll out a thin piece of fondant and cut out the flap, using the measurements shown (Figure 3). Dip a small paintbrush in water and brush the top of the cake in the area where the flap will lie. Lay the flap on top of the cake, pressing it gently to the cake (Figure 4).

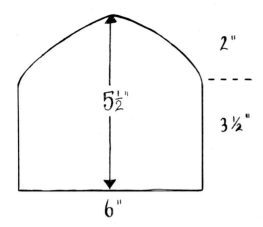

2"

5½"

3½"

6"

Figure 3

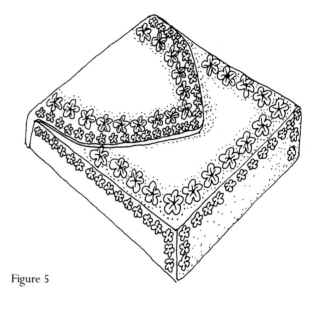

Figure 5

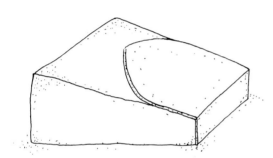

Figure 4

With the small flower-shaped cutters, emboss a border of flowers around the edge of the flap, the top edge of the cake and the bottom and sides of the cake. Emboss dots around the flowers with a round toothpick (Figure 5).

Pipe a shell border with the #14 tip and peach-colored royal icing around the edge of the flap and the top, bottom, and side "seams" of the purse.

Place the run-in sugar circle on the tip of the flap to make the clasp.

To make the gold rope handle, divide the remaining fondant into two equal pieces. Roll out two ropes of icing, each ¼ inch thick. Twist the two ropes together to form a single rope. Roll the rope a few times to press the two ropes to each other. Attach the two ends of the rope to the back of the cake, on either side of the top of the purse, with a little water. Paint the rope with gold powder mixed with a little lemon extract.

Fabergé Jewelry Box

This cake was inspired by a design by Fabergé. The dragees give it a jeweled look and you can personalize it by adding the initial of the recipient onto the top of the cake.

Serves 15

Cakes:

5x7-inch rectangle, 1 inch high
5x7-inch rectangle, 2 inches high (each cake is
    made from a 7-inch square, and cut to size)

1 recipe rolled fondant
sewing needle and dental floss
waxed paper
1 recipe royal icing
blue rock candy
blue, gold, and silver dragees
white iridescent and gold edible powders
lemon extract
1 recipe buttercream icing
5x7-inch foam board
ruler
silver platter or 9-inch round foam board, covered
    with silver foil
green paste food coloring
tips #2, #14

In advance:

Make the rolled fondant. For the string of pearls, set aside about ½ cup of fondant. Tint the rest of the fondant pale green. Wrap the green fondant in plastic wrap and place in an airtight container. Roll the white fondant into twenty-six ⅝-inch balls. Set the balls on a paper towel to dry for twenty-four hours. After the balls have set, thread a needle with a 10-inch piece of doubled dental floss and string the balls on the thread. Tie a knot and set aside.

To make the run-in sugar pin, draw a 2-inch circle on a piece of paper. Tape a piece of waxed paper over the circle. Mix a tablespoon of royal icing with a little water to make the icing runny. Pipe the thinned icing with the #2 tip onto the 2-inch circle. The icing will spread a bit after it is placed on the paper, so make the icing circle a little smaller than you need it to be. Let the circle dry for twenty-four hours.

Crumble a piece of blue rock candy into small pieces. Pipe a large dot of royal icing in the center of the dry run-in circle and place a large piece of rock candy in the center of the dot. Pipe a thin line of royal icing around the center dot and place silver dragees in a circle in the icing. Coat the rest of the circle with royal icing and sprinkle the rock candy in the icing to cover the circle. Set aside to dry.

To make the two gold earrings, pipe two circular stars on a piece of waxed paper with white royal icing, using the #14 tip. Make the circles about ¾ inch wide (Figure 1). Set these aside to dry. When the icing has dried, paint with gold powder mixed with a little lemon extract.

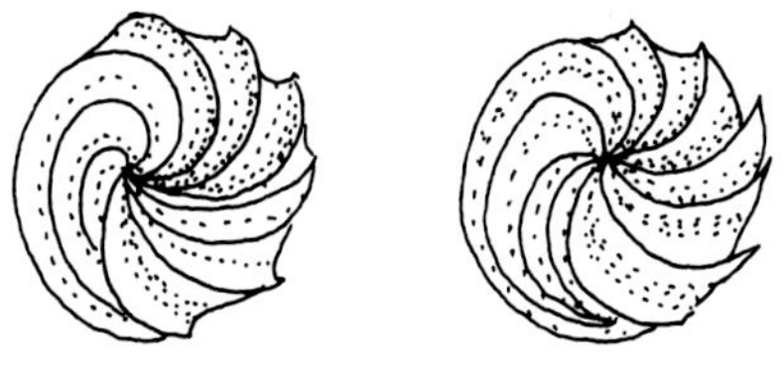

Figure 1

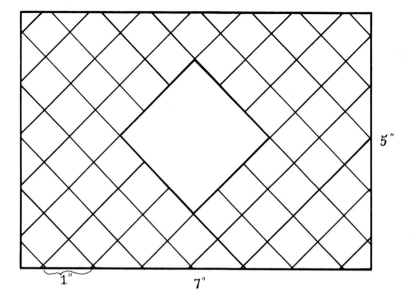

Figure 2

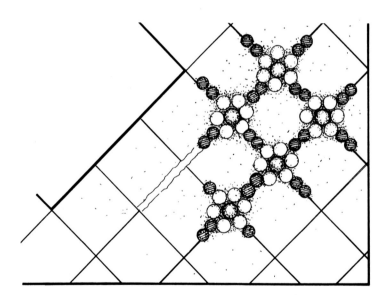

Figure 3

To decorate the cake:

Bake the cakes and allow them to cool. Place the 1-inch-high rectangular layer on the 5x7-inch foam board. Place the other layer on a platter, using a little buttercream to secure it. Cover both cakes with buttercream and then with light green fondant.

Mark the top of the 1-inch-high layer with diagonal lines, using a toothpick and ruler (Figure 2). Paint the large center diamond with white iridescent powder mixed with a few drops of lemon extract.

Pipe a shell border around the edge of the large diamond in the center of the cake. Place silver dragees at the four intersections of the shells. Along the lines marked on the cake, pipe thin lines of white royal icing, using the #2 tip. Place blue dragees end to end on the piped lines while the icing is wet. Work on a small area at a time, as the icing tends to dry quickly. Pipe a small dot of icing at each intersection and place a gold dragee in the icing. Pipe a circle of icing around the gold dragee and place a ring of 6 silver dragees in the icing (Figure 3).

In the center of the large diamond, pipe the initial of the person in whose honor the cake is being made (Figure 4, on page 64). Insert silver dragees in the icing.

Pipe a shell border around the top edge of the cake and insert silver dragees into the icing between each shell. Set this layer aside to dry.

To decorate the bottom layer, pipe a shell border with white royal icing around the base of the cake and the top edge. Place silver dragees in between each of the shells and a blue dragee between the silver dragees. Pipe a triple row of shells vertically up each corner of the cake. Place silver dragees between the shells in the middle row, and blue dragees in between the shells on the outside rows.

Place the string of pearls on top of the bottom layer, so that the pearls hang down onto the platter. Use a little royal icing to hold them in place.

To make a silver necklace, pipe a loop of royal icing in the corner of the cake and place a line of silver dragees in the icing.

Pipe a thick line of royal icing along one 7-inch side of the top of the bottom layer. Place the smaller layer on top of the bottom layer, setting the back of the lid in the royal icing to hold it in place. The string of pearls will keep the lid slightly upright.

Pipe a white royal icing shell border around the bottom edge of the lid and place gold dragees in between the shells.

Place the run-in sugar "jewel" and the 2 earrings on the platter. Fabergé himself could not have done it better.

Indian Beaded Cake

The design for this cake was inspired by the beadwork of the Southwestern American Indians. I used small bead-like candies, which can be found in bulk candy stores. As a substitute for the candies, dots of buttercream icing can be piped from a #4 round tip, in the various colors indicated.

Serves 20

8-inch round cake, 4 inches high (2 layers)
yellow, blue, red, green, orange, and black bead
       candies, ¼ inch in diameter
1 recipe yellow buttercream icing
14-inch round platter
yellow paste food coloring
tip #4

To decorate the cake:

Bake the cakes and let them cool completely. Place the bottom layer on a 14-inch plate. Add filling and the top layer. Cover the cake with yellow buttercream.

Start decorating the cake from the top center outward, and then work down the sides when the top is finished. Find the center of the cake, as described in the section on marking divisions on a cake, page 13. This is the point where you will start the beadwork.

Using the #4 tip and yellow buttercream icing, pipe a small dot in the center and place a blue bead in the icing. Next, pipe seven dots of

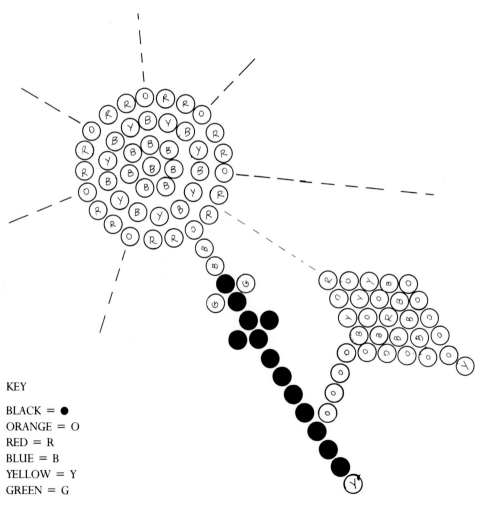

KEY

BLACK = ●
ORANGE = O
RED = R
BLUE = B
YELLOW = Y
GREEN = G

Figure 1

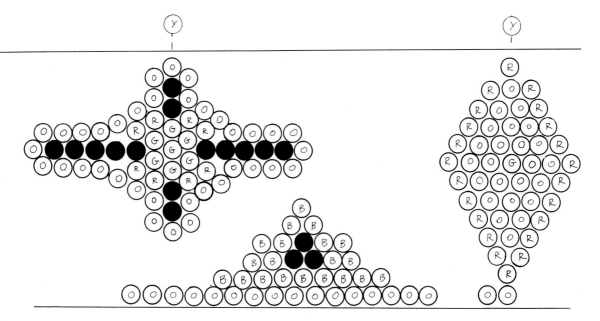

Figure 2

icing in a circle around the center bead and place seven blue beads around the first bead. Place all of the beads up against each other so that the cake does not show through.

The design on the top of the cake is divided into seven sections, each section radiating from the first circle of beads. Continue adding the beads with icing, following the diagram (Figure 1). All of the spaces between the design illustrated are filled in with yellow beads.

When the top of the cake is completely covered, start working down the sides of the cake. The designs on the side of the cake should line up with the designs on the top (Figure 2).

To complete the cake, pipe thin lines of icing onto the plate and add beads as a fringe.

Part
III

Intermediate
Cakes

The Baby's Bib

I made this cake for a baby shower for a friend of mine. Since no one knew ahead of time if the baby was a boy or a girl, I decided to make the colors peach and purple. Everyone will think you spent weeks knitting until they cut into this adorable cake.

Serves 35

12-inch round cake, 2 inches high
1 recipe royal icing
waxed paper
1 recipe white buttercream icing
ruler or straightedge
16-inch platter
yellow, pink, and purple paste food coloring
tips #2, two #3s, #15, #18, #44, #104

In advance:

Make the loops and ribbons for the bow on waxed paper with white royal icing, using the #104 tip (see page 21). Make two loops about 2½ inches long and two ribbon ends about 4 inches long. Make a few extra in case of breakage. Set aside to dry for twenty-four hours.

To make the run-in sugar animals, trace the patterns provided onto a piece of paper (Figures 1, 2, and 3). Place a piece of waxed paper over the tracings and tape it onto a board or cookie sheet. On the waxed paper, outline the rabbit and the bear with stiff white icing with the #2 tip. Tint a small amount of icing pink to outline the duck. Fill in the rabbit with thinned white icing, using the #2 tip. Do the same with the bear and the duck, tinting the icing a pale purple for the bear and yellow for the duck. Set these aside to dry.

After a few hours, go back and add eyes, noses, ears, and a bow on the bear with stiff white icing from the #2 tip and the wing on the duck with stiff pink royal icing from the #2 tip. Let the figures dry for at least twenty-four hours.

Figure 1

Figure 2

Figure 3

To decorate the cake:

Bake the cake and cool. Cut a 5½-inch round hole, 1 inch in from one edge. Carefully remove the cut-out section. Place the cake on a platter, with a dab of icing to secure it, and coat the cake, including the inside of the hole, with thinned white buttercream icing. When the icing has set, coat the cake with a thicker coat of icing.

Tint about 1 cup of buttercream a peach color, using pink and a little yellow. Tint ½ cup of buttercream pale yellow. You will need two #3 tips and two decorating bags, one for each color.

Take a clean ruler or straightedge and lightly mark the cake, using a toothpick, with straight vertical lines to use as a guide when piping the knitted loops. Start at the left edge of the cake and make two rows of peach-colored loops, overlapping the loops (Figure 4). Then make a row of yellow loops. Continue to alternate two rows of peach loops and one row of yellow until the top of the cake is covered (Figure 5).

Pipe a shell border of white buttercream inside the bottom edge of the cut-out hole and around the outer edge of the base of the cake, using the #18 tip.

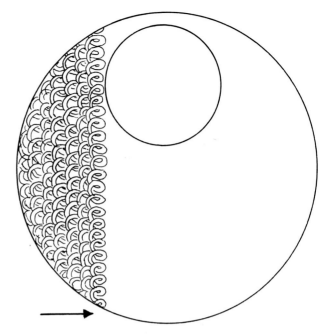

Figure 5

To make the ruffle edges, use a #104 tip and white buttercream. Make the ruffle around the edge of the hole first by placing the wide end of the tip to the inside of the hole and the thin edge facing toward the outside. Pipe the ruffle using a slight up-and-down motion as you pipe (Figure 6).

Figure 4

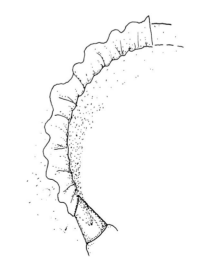

Figure 6

The ruffle on the outer edge of the cake is piped with the #104 tip in the same manner as a daisy petal (Figure 7).

Pipe small white stars around the inside edge of the large ruffle with the #15 star tip.

Pipe drop strings using the #3 tip along the outer edge of the larger ruffled border. Pipe a second row of drop strings, starting in the center of each string (Figure 8).

Tint a small amount of buttercream pale purple and pipe a dotted line with the #44 tip, making the lines about ½ inch long, to give the illusion of a ribbon. Pipe the purple lines parallel to the inside and outside ruffles.

Attach the three run-in sugar animals to the cake with a dab of buttercream.

Finally, attach the bow to the top of the cake with white buttercream icing. Pipe a mound of icing onto the cake and place the ends of the

Figure 7

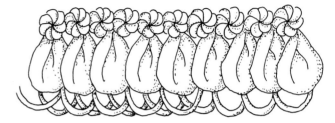

Figure 8

ribbons in the icing. Pipe a little more icing to attach the bows. Pipe a center ribbon to connect the loops, using the #104 tip.

Irish Lace

The delicate pattern on this cake makes it appear as if a lace doily has been placed on it. The idea for the cake came from a book of lace designs. It's the perfect cake for a young girl's birthday party or an afternoon tea. It takes a lot of patience, but the results are worth the effort.

Serves 20

8-inch round cake, 4 inches high (2 layers)
1 recipe buttercream icing
1 recipe rolled fondant
1 recipe royal icing
1 pink royal icing rose
2 green royal icing leaves
2 12-inch scalloped boards (available at
    cake-decorating stores), glued together
compass
ruler
pink paste food coloring
tip #2

In advance:

Make the royal icing rose and leaves (see pages 15–16 and 20–21).

Make the rolled fondant and tint it a pale pink. Wrap it in plastic wrap and place in an airtight plastic bag and allow it to set overnight at room temperature.

To decorate the cake:

Bake the cakes and cool. Place the bottom layer on the board, securing it with a dab of buttercream. Add filling and then the top layer.

Cover the cake with buttercream.

Roll out the fondant until it is large enough to cover the cake and board. Place the fondant on the cake and smooth it down the sides of the cake, working it down to the edges of the board. Cut off the excess fondant around the scalloped edge. Ease the fondant over the edges of the scallops.

Draw an 8-inch circle with a compass on a piece of paper. Divide the circle into seven equal pieces by using the angle shown (Figure 1). Cut out the circle and lay it on top of the cake. Mark the center of the cake with a

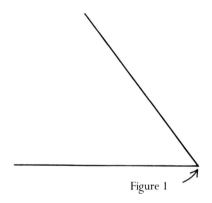

Figure 1

toothpick through the hole in the center of the paper. Mark the seven sections of the circle on top of the cake. Then, lay a straightedge on the cake and make dots with a toothpick along the seven radiating lines from the center of the cake to the outer marks.

Lay a ruler along one of the seven radius divisions on the paper circle and make a pencil

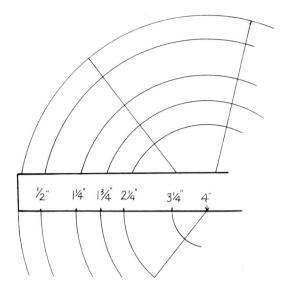

Figure 2

Repeat the same process described above, cutting the circle and marking the cake after each cut, until the final circle is 1½ inches in diameter.

Mark the scallops on the cake with a toothpick, using the concentric circles on the cake as a guide (Figure 3).

Pipe lines along the outlines of the scallops' edges and the seven radius lines with the #2 tip and white royal icing.

Pipe evenly spaced lines inside each scallop (Figure 4). Rather than dragging the icing along the surface of the cake, which will give you a bumpy line, allow the icing to attach to the piped outline and then slightly lift the tip up off the edge of the cake as the icing flows from the tip. Lay the tip down to attach the end of the line to the center point of the scallop. This will give a clean, straight string of icing and a much better appearance.

Pipe a line ¼ inch in and parallel to the outline of the outermost large scallop.

Outline all of the scallops with a piped loop line.

Pipe dots at the points of all of the scallops.

Pipe a looped line around the outer edge of the top of the cake.

mark at ½ inch, 1¼ inches, 1¾ inches, 2¼ inches, and 3¼ inches, marking from the outer edge to the center dot. Make concentric circles with the compass through each of the marks (Figure 2).

Cut the paper around the first concentric circle, which is ½ inch in from the outer edge. Lay the paper on the cake and make toothpick dots along the circumference of the circle.

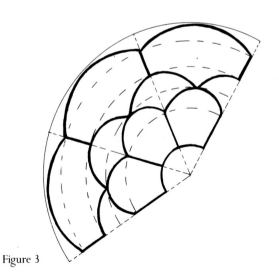

Figure 3

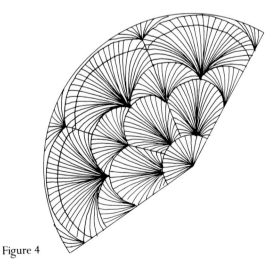

Figure 4

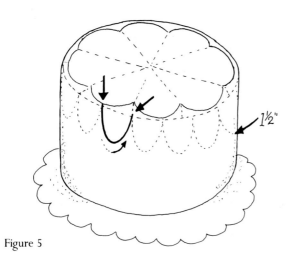

Figure 5

Next, pipe the designs for the side of the cake. The design on the top of the cake will act as a guide as to where to start the designs on the side. Make toothpick marks 1½ inches from the top of the cake down the side. Start the first drop-string arch at the center of the outer edge of the large scallop on the top of the cake. Let the string drop down 1½ inches and end the string at the outer edge of the intersection of the 2 large scallops (Figure 5). Continue to make drop-string arches all around the side of the cake.

Pipe nine lines inside each of the arches, starting the line at the outline of the arch and piping upward to the center of the arch (Figure 6).

Pipe a curved horizontal line between the large arches and add two vertical curved lines inside the small curves (Figure 7).

Pipe five tassel lines from the center of the small arch extending about 2 inches down (Figure 8).

Pipe a looped outline all around the arches and at the top of the tassel. Pipe six dots at the bottom of each of the large arches and dots at the points of the arches (Figure 9).

Pipe a horizontal double row of small scallops ¾ inches up from the bottom of the cake.

Make the arches on the scalloped base of the cake using the same procedure as the design on the side of the cake, except you will eliminate the step in Figure 8. Instead, a tassel is piped in between the large arches. Make each arch parallel to the outer arch of the base. The arches should be about 1 inch out from the bottom of the cake.

Pipe three rows of drop-string arches starting and ending at the top row of small scallops ¾ inch up from the bottom of the cake.

The finishing touch: attach the two royal icing leaves and the rose to the center of the cake with a dab of icing.

Figure 6

Figure 7

Figure 8

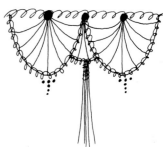

Figure 9

Chinese Dragon

I designed this cake for the owner of a Chinese travel agency. The dragon is the logo for his company and also a symbol of good luck. Good luck creating this scary dragon for the Chinese New Year.

Serves 60

Cakes:

12-inch round, 3 inches high (2 layers)
10-inch round, 2 inches high

2 recipes rolled fondant
2 recipes buttercream icing
16-inch round foam board, 2 layers thick, covered with red foil
corn syrup
10-inch round foam board
sharp X-acto knife
unsweetened cocoa powder
clear piping gel
gold edible powder
red liquid food coloring, yellow paste coloring
tips #1, #3, #18

In advance:

Make the rolled fondant and let it set for twenty-four hours at room temperature wrapped in plastic and placed in an airtight container.

To decorate the cake:

Bake and cool the cakes. Freeze the 10-inch layer, wrapped in foil, for a few hours. This will make it easier to cut, with less crumbling.

Place the 12-inch layers on the 16-inch board, with filling in between the layers, using a dab of buttercream to secure the cake to the board. Cover the cake with buttercream and then cover it with rolled fondant. Since it would be impossible to get the fondant bright red by kneading in red coloring, paint the surface of the cake with red liquid coloring until it is bright red. Let it dry. Then paint the surface of the cake with corn syrup thinned with a little water to give it a sheen. Let the syrup dry.

Trace the pattern for the dragon on a piece of paper. Then place the pattern for the dragon on top of the 10-inch board. Outline the pattern onto the board and carefully cut out the shape with a sharp X-acto knife (Figure 1, page 81). Spread a layer of buttercream on the shaped board and lay the board iced side down on the 10-inch cake. Using a serrated knife, cut out the cake around the board. Turn the cake and board over. Remove the cake that is not attached to the board. Round off all of the edges of the cake.

Cover the dragon with thinned buttercream. It will probably take two coats to get the dragon's surface smooth. Add the second coat of buttercream after the first coat has dried.

Tint the remaining fondant yellow. Roll out the fondant until it is about 2 inches larger on all sides than the dragon. Place the pattern for the dragon on the fondant and cut around the outside of the shape, leaving 1 inch extra all around. Do not cut the inside pieces yet. Care-

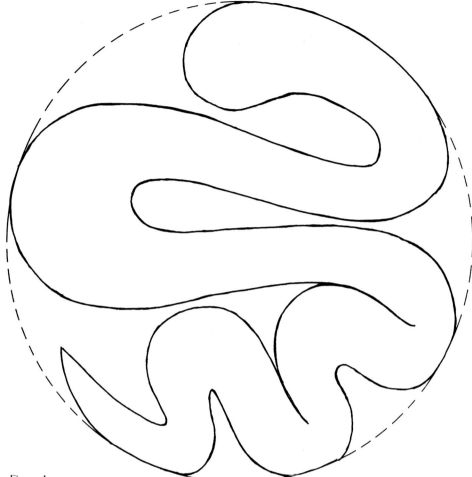

Figure 1

fully lay the fondant over the dragon cake and ease the fondant down into the cut-out areas. Trim off the excess fondant around the base of the dragon.

Trim the excess fondant inside the dragon. Lay the dragon centered on top of the bottom layer, using a dab of buttercream to hold it in place.

With a toothpick, mark a line running along the center of the length of the dragon's body (Figure 2, page 83). On the left side of this dividing line, make curved lines with the tooth-

pick to make the scales for the belly of the dragon (Figure 3, page 83). On the other side of the dividing line, make scales with the back of a decorating tip (Figure 4, page 83).

Roll out a strip of fondant 1½ inches wide and as long as the back of the dragon. Cut triangular wedges out of the strip at 1-inch intervals (Figure 5, page 82). Brush the bottom edge of the back of the dragon with a little water and attach the jagged-edged strip.

Cut a piece of fondant using the pattern for the arm (Figure 6, page 82). Brush the cake with water in the area for the arm and attach the fondant arm. Add scales to the arm as in Figure 4.

Roll out five small cones of fondant, about ¾ inches long and ¼ inch wide. These will make the five fingers of the dragon. Attach the fingers with a little water, using the diagram for placement.

Roll out ten cones of fondant about 2 inches long and very thin. Place these in back of the head for the hair, with a little water. If they start to sag, place little wads of paper toweling in between the pieces until they set (Figure 7).

Roll out two small balls of fondant to make the nostrils. These should be about ¼ inch wide. Form the balls into small rectangles and place on the front of the head with a little water (Figure 8).

Add two long cones to the front of the face for the whiskers.

Pipe small white dots of buttercream, using the #3 tip, along the scales of the belly. Outline the triangles on the back of the dragon and the hair with thin white buttercream lines. Outline the fingers and the whiskers with white buttercream lines.

Tint a half cup of buttercream bright red and another half cup bright orange. Pipe a line of each color with a #3 tip along the top length of the dragon, using a continuous loop motion. Pipe a red and orange line inside each of the triangles on the back of the dragon. Pipe a double line of red and orange along the bottom edge of the entire dragon, using the same loop motion.

Figure 6

Pipe a red dot for the eye and red inside of the mouth.

Pipe orange eyebrows and a line around the mouth. Pipe a red outline around the orange line of the mouth. Pipe white teeth with the #3 tip, attaching the icing to the mouth by applying pressure to the bag and then pulling the icing out to a point as the icing flows from the tip.

Mix about ¼ teaspoon gold powder with about 2 tablespoons of clear piping gel. Place the gel in a pastry bag and attach the #1 tip. Outline the arm, whiskers, hair, triangles, and mouth with thin gold lines. Pipe tiny dots along the top length of the dragon and a dot in each eye. Pipe lines on the fingers.

Set aside a half cup of the white buttercream and mix the rest of the icing with cocoa until it becomes dark brown. If the icing is too thick, add a little hot water to thin. Fill a pastry bag with the chocolate icing and fit on the #18 tip. Fit the #3 tip onto a bag containing the white icing.

Pipe elongated shells with the chocolate icing around the base of the cake, on the board. Pipe elongated shells on the side of the cake, just above the first set of shells.

Pipe a thin white outline around the curved part of the chocolate shells.

Pipe tiny gold dots on the side of the cake with the gold piping gel.

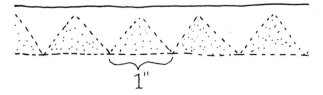
1"

Figure 5

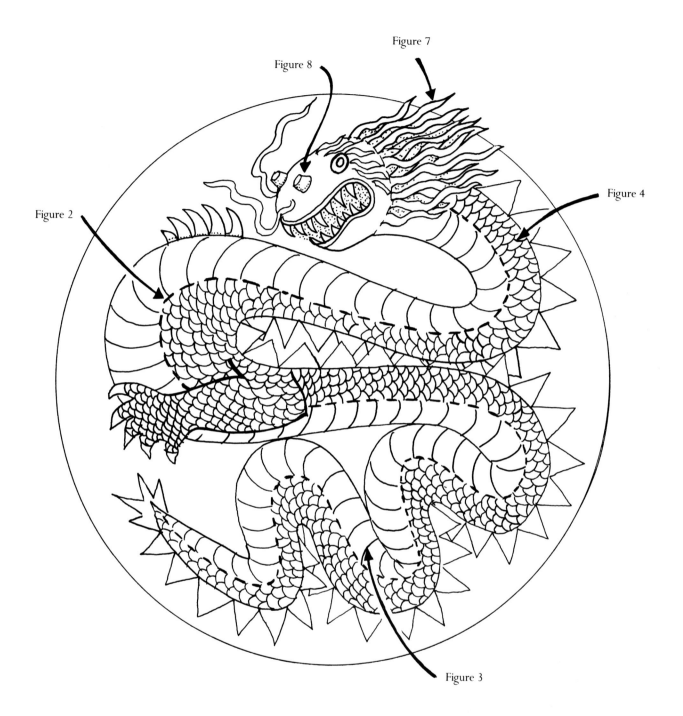

Figure 7

Figure 8

Figure 4

Figure 2

Figure 3

Spring Bouquet

This cake was created for a wedding shower, to match the bride's bouquet. You can also use this cake for a wedding by baking it in a large metal bowl and increasing the number of flowers.

Serves 10

Cakes:

half of a 6-inch ball
6-inch round, 2 inches high

Toothpick flowers:

5 large orange lilies (page 18)
3 large white lilies (page 18)
10 red carnations (page 16)
20 assorted pink, white, and lavender roses (pages 15–16)
10 pink and white daisies (page 15)
10 small yellow chrysanthemums (page 17)
25 leaves (pages 20–21)

Wired flowers:

14 purple hyacinths (page 19)
14 heather (page 19)
60 single yellow baby's breath blossoms made with tip #15 (page 19)

8-inch round foam board, covered with foil
1 yard of 2½-inch-wide white lace
7-inch round foam board, covered with foil
3 yards of assorted ribbon
white cloth-covered wire
green florist tape
1 recipe basic buttercream icing, tinted green
tip #69

In advance:

Make all of the flowers and allow them to dry at least twenty-four hours. Cover the wire stems with florist tape.

Cover the 8-inch board with foil. To give the board a ruffled lace edge, tape or staple one edge of the lace around the circumference of the board, ½ inch in from the outer edge of the board. Cut off the excess lace.

To make the cluster of ribbons, make a 2-inch loop in the center of the ribbon, letting the ends extend about 8 inches (Figure 1). Gather together about fifteen loops and tie them together at the base of the loops with a thin white wire, allowing the end of the wire to extend out about 2 inches (Figure 2). Wrap the end of the wire in florist tape.

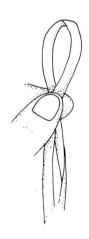

Figure 1

Figure 2

To decorate the cake:

Bake the cakes and cool completely. Attach the 6-inch layer to the covered 7-inch board with a dab of buttercream. Add filling and place the 6-inch ball on top of the bottom layer. Cover the cake with green buttercream. Attach the 7-inch board to the 8-inch board with buttercream.

Insert the wire extending from the ribbon cluster into the front of the cake. Start placing flowers and leaves into the bottom edge of the cake. With the #69 tip, pipe green buttercream leaves around the base of the flowers and leaves (Figure 3). Cover the entire surface of the cake with flowers and leaves.

Figure 3

Blue Hawaii

The idea for this cake came from a fabric pattern. It's great for a party with a Hawaiian theme. The leaves and flowers are all piped on the cake, except for the top decorations.

Serves 55

Cakes:

8-inch round, 4 inches high (2 layers)
10-inch round, 4 inches high (2 layers)

1 recipe royal icing
12-inch round foam board, 3 layers thick
waxed paper
3 recipes pure white basic buttercream icing
half of a 4-inch Styrofoam ball
8-inch and 10-inch round foam boards
sky blue, purple, pink, yellow, and kelly green
    paste food colors
tips #4, #18, #65, #352

In advance:

To prepare the board, tint 1½ cups of royal icing with sky blue food coloring. Thin ½ cup of the icing with water until it reaches the consistency of syrup. Spread the icing on the triple-thickness 12-inch board until smooth and set the board on a piece of waxed paper that is larger than the board. Pipe a shell border all around the edge of the board with the #18 tip and the remaining stiff blue icing. Set aside to dry for at least twenty-four hours.

Take the remaining white royal icing and set aside ¼ cup for the white outlines. Tint ¼ cup of the icing a deep purple. Tint another ½ cup of the icing bright pink. Divide the remaining

icing into two parts and tint one part bright green and the other bright yellow. On a piece of waxed paper, pipe sixteen 2-inch-long green and sixteen yellow leaves with the #352 tip. Pipe seven 6-petaled pink flowers (Figure 1). Pipe six 3-petaled purple flowers with the #65 tip (Figure 2). Let these set for a few hours, and then outline all of the flowers and leaves with the white icing, using the #4 tip. Pipe small white dots in the center of all of the purple flowers and yellow dots in the center of the pink flowers. Let these dry overnight.

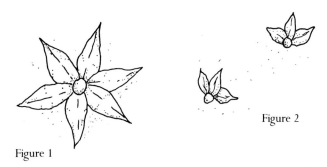

Figure 1

Figure 2

Make the buttercream icing. It should be pure white (made with shortening) so that the blue coloring stays a true blue. If butter or margarine is used, the icing will have a greenish look when the blue coloring is added. Tint about 3 cups of the buttercream sky blue. Leave 1 cup of the buttercream white. Tint 1 cup of the icing bright yellow, ¾ cup bright pink, and the remaining icing purple. Green will be made with the remaining blue icing after the cake is iced.

Tint the buttercream a shade lighter than the royal icing colors, because buttercream icing gets darker as it dries. The buttercream should be tinted one day in advance so that the colors have time to set.

To decorate the cake:

Bake all of the cakes and allow to cool. Place the respective tiers on the 8-inch and 10-inch foam boards, attaching them with a dab of buttercream. Ice smoothly with the blue buttercream and stack the cakes on the prepared blue board, with dowels in the bottom tier as described in the section on tiered cakes in Part I.

Cut a 4-inch Styrofoam ball in half and cut out a circle of waxed paper the same size as the bottom of the ball. Attach the waxed paper circle to the bottom of the ball with a dab of buttercream. (The waxed paper prevents the Styrofoam from touching the top of the cake.)

Ice the ball with blue buttercream and attach it to the top of the cake with a dab of buttercream.

Pipe white stems on the cake using the #4 tip, using the photograph as a guide. These are primarily piped diagonally around the cake.

Using the #352 tip, pipe yellow and green buttercream leaves along the stems. Pipe randomly placed pink flowers with the same tip. Pipe small yellow dots in the center of the pink flowers. With the #65 tip, pipe purple 3-petaled flowers and pipe small white dots in the centers.

Attach the dried royal icing leaves and flowers to the Styrofoam ball with blue buttercream, using the #18 tip.

Finally, go back with the white buttercream and the #4 tip and outline all of the leaves and flowers on the cake.

Holly Cake

This cake was designed for the Tiffany & Company Christmas catalog. Its simplicity and elegance make this a lovely cake for any winter holiday table.

Serves 20

8-inch round cake, 4 inches high (2 layers)
1 recipe gum paste
1 recipe royal icing
waxed paper
toothpicks
1 recipe rolled fondant
plastic or marble cutting board
small rolling pin
foam rubber
holly leaf gum paste cutter
small paintbrush
1 recipe buttercream icing
50 small red candy balls
kelly green paste food coloring
12-inch cake stand
tips #3, #32, #66

In advance:

Make a recipe of gum paste and add green paste food coloring until a deep green color is reached. Let it set for twenty-four hours at room temperature in an airtight plastic bag.

After the gum paste has set, roll it out onto a plastic or marble cutting board following the directions for gum paste bows (pages 22–23). Cut out holly leaves with the holly cutter. Cut only a few leaves at a time so that the gum paste does not dry out. (Hint: Place the gum paste under an upside-down glass while you are working to keep it from drying out.) You will need a total of forty leaves. Place the cut-out leaves on a piece of foam rubber and score each leaf with a toothpick to make the veins (Figure 1). Place the leaves on a paper towel to dry. Curve the leaves slightly while still pliable to give them a natural look (Figure 2). Allow them to dry for twenty-four hours.

When the leaves are completely dry, brush them with a small amount of vegetable shortening or cooking oil to give the leaves a sheen.

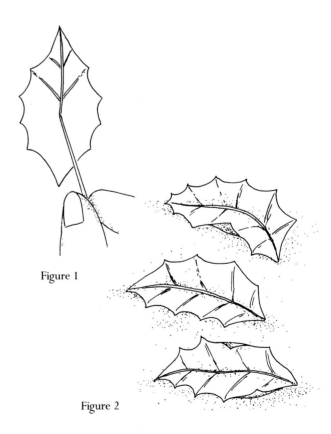

Figure 1

Figure 2

Figure 3   Figure 4

Make a recipe of royal icing and add green coloring until it is dark green. Pipe a leaf with the #66 tip onto a piece of waxed paper (Figure 3). Take a small, damp paintbrush and pull the brush from the center of the leaf out to the edge of the leaf along the vein lines to form a point. This must be done while the icing is still wet (Figure 4). Make sixteen leaves in this way and let them dry for twenty-four hours.

Make the rolled fondant, wrap it in plastic, and put it in an airtight plastic bag. Let it set at room temperature overnight.

To decorate the cake:

Bake the cake and let it cool. Place the bottom layer on a 12-inch cake stand, using a dab of buttercream to hold it in place. Add the filling and the top layer. Cover with buttercream and then with rolled fondant.

Outline the bottom of the 8-inch cake pan on a piece of paper. Cut out the circle and fold it into sixteen sections. Place the paper circle on top of the cake and mark the sixteen sections along the circumference with a toothpick.

Using white buttercream icing and the #3 tip, pipe three drop strings between each mark on the cake, the longest string measuring 1½ inches down from the top of the cake. Pipe a loop on either side of the tops of the strings to form a bow. Place a red candy in the center of the bow. Cover the top of the cake with white dots.

Pipe a mound of white buttercream in the center of the cake. Place six of the gum paste holly leaves in the wet icing and place candy balls around the leaves in the icing.

Attach the sixteen royal icing leaves to the intersection of the drop strings with a dab of buttercream.

Pipe a large shell border around the base of the cake with buttercream, using the #32 tip. Insert the end of a holly leaf in between each shell. Attach red candies around the holly leaves.

Christmas Tree Centerpiece

The kids will love helping you create this holiday decoration. It's easy because there is no baking involved. You can use the specific candies indicated here, or you can use your imagination at the candy store and create your own combinations to decorate the tree. If stored in a plastic bag in a cool, dry place, your tree can be used for many years.

18-inch Styrofoam cone with an 8-inch base
23 red royal icing poinsettias (page 18) with 3 gold dragees in the center of each
8 red royal icing bows
waxed paper
gold and large silver dragees
2 recipes royal icing
35 rectangular sugar cubes
12-inch round foam board, covered with foil or Christmas wrapping
assorted red and white candies, such as small candy canes, Lifesavers, peppermints, gumdrops, gummy bells, and red M&Ms
red paste food coloring
tips #3, #14, #18

In advance:

Make all of the poinsettias and let them dry for at least twenty-four hours.

For the red bows and the sugar cube packages, tint about ½ cup of royal icing a deep red. Make the eight bows on waxed paper using the #14 tip. Make two loops, piping in a figure-eight motion (Figure 1). Then pipe the two ribbons below the loops (Figure 2). The

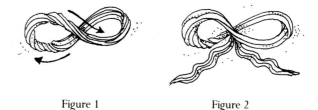

Figure 1   Figure 2

bows should be about 2 inches wide. Make a few extra in case of breakage. Set these aside and allow to dry overnight.

Next, decorate the sugar cube packages. Use the #3 tip and red royal icing. The easiest way to work with the sugar cubes is to hold the cube in one hand and to pipe with the other. This way you can work on all sides of the cube at once, and it makes it easier to control where you want the icing to go. You can decorate these in a variety of ways (Figure 3). Make about thirty-five packages and set them aside to dry.

When the royal icing decorations are dry, start to set up your tree. Cover a 12-inch

Figure 3

round foam board with red foil or Christmas wrapping paper. Fit a pastry bag with the #18 tip and fill with white royal icing. Pipe some icing on the bottom of the Styrofoam cone and set it in the center of the board. Measure ½ inch up from the bottom of the cone to leave room for the sugar cube packages. You will be decorating the tree from the bottom up.

Pipe a circle of icing on the back of a poinsettia and glue it on around the bottom of the tree above the ½-inch mark. Add a total of ten poinsettias, spaced evenly, around the bottom. Glue large silver dragees in between all the poinsettias. (All of the decorations are "glued" with white royal icing.)

The following is a list of the candies in the order in which they are attached to the tree, after you have attached the first row of poinsettias:

1. Peppermint candies with a dragee in each center
2. Red gumdrops
3. Red M&Ms alternating with peppermints with dragee centers
4. Eight red bows
5. Small candy canes
6. Silver dragees
7. Seven poinsettias
8. Peppermint candies with dragee centers
9. Red gummy bells
10. Seven sugar cube packages
11. Red Lifesavers with a piped white bow
12. Red gumdrops
13. Five poinsettias
14. Nine 2-inch-long peppermint candy sticks
15. Silver dragees
16. Red hearts
17. One poinsettia on the top

To finish the tree, pipe branches all over the tree using the white royal icing and the #18 tip. Place the tip against the cone and squeeze out a small amount of icing. Put more pressure on the bag and then pull out and down so that the icing comes to a point (Figure 4).

Glue the sugar cube packages around the base of the tree with royal icing. Allow the tree to dry for at least twenty-four hours.

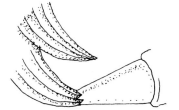

Figure 4

New Year's Eve Cake

The gold run-in sugar clock face on the top of the cake will tell everyone that the new year is fast approaching.

Serves 25

9-inch round cake, 4 inches high (2 layers)
11 large white royal icing poinsettias (page 18)
waxed paper
1 recipe royal icing
1 recipe rolled fondant
1 recipe white buttercream icing
edible gold powder
lemon extract
small paintbrush
candy confetti
gold dragees
9-inch round foam board
13-inch round foam board, 2 layers thick
½-inch gold ribbon to cover the edge of the board
tips #2, #3, #4, #13, #69

In advance:

Make the poinsettias and place three gold dragees in the center of each. Set these aside to dry for two days.

Make the hands of the clock using the patterns provided (Figure 1). Trace the patterns onto a piece of paper and place a sheet of waxed paper over the tracing. Pipe the stems of the hands with stiff white royal icing, using the #4 tip. Outline the ends of the hands with the #2 tip and fill in with run-in icing (see page 8). Let these dry for twenty-four hours.

Make the twelve discs using white run-in sugar. First, draw twelve circles, 1⅝ inches

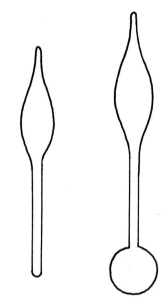

Figure 1

wide, on a piece of paper. Tape a piece of waxed paper over the paper patterns. Pipe a thin outline around the circumference of each circle with stiff icing and then fill in the circles with thinned icing. Let the discs dry for twenty-four hours.

Draw twelve 1-inch squares on a piece of paper. Draw the numerals in the squares (Figure 2, on page 98). Place a piece of waxed paper over the paper and tape it down. Pipe the roman numerals with stiff royal icing on the waxed paper, using the #4 tip. Make extra in case of breakage. Let the numerals dry for twenty-four hours.

When all of your decorations have dried,

Figure 2

paint the hands of the clock and the numerals gold, using about ¼ teaspoon of gold powder mixed with a few drops of lemon extract. Use a small paintbrush and gently brush the paint onto the designs. Allow the paint to dry.

Carefully remove the numerals from the waxed paper by gently sliding a metal spatula underneath each numeral. Attach the numerals to the centers of each run-in sugar disc with a thin line of royal icing piped on the back of the numerals. Pipe a thin shell border with white royal icing around the circumference of each disc with the #13 tip. Let dry.

Cover the 13-inch double-thickness board with thinned royal icing. Wrap a gold ribbon around the edge of the board when the icing is dry.

Make the rolled fondant and wrap in plastic and place in an airtight plastic bag. Let it set overnight at room temperature.

To decorate the cake:

Bake the cakes and allow them to cool. When cooled, place the layers on the 9-inch board, with filling in between. Cover with buttercream icing and then with fondant. Place the cake on the prepared board.

Pipe a mound of buttercream icing at the base of the front of the cake and set a poinsettia in the icing. Place all of the poinsettias, evenly spaced, around the bottom of the cake. Pipe white buttercream leaves in between the flowers, using the #69 tip.

Next, arrange the run-in sugar discs on the top of the cake, evenly spaced in a circle. Secure the discs to the top of the cake with a small dab of buttercream. Pipe a thin line of icing on the backs of the hands of the clock and place them in the center of the cake so that they are almost at 12 o'clock.

Pipe the drop-string edge around the top of the cake, using the #3 tip and white buttercream. Use the twelve discs on the top of the cake as your guides as to where to start the strings. Start the first set of three strings between and slightly below the intersections of two of the discs. Pipe a triple row of strings, the longest string measuring down 1½ inches. Pipe a loop at the top of the point where the three strings meet (Figure 3). Next, pipe a dou-

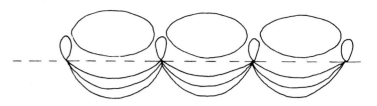

Figure 3

ble row of strings, starting in the center of the three previous strings. Pipe eight dots above the first three strings (Figure 4).

Sprinkle the cake with candy confetti.

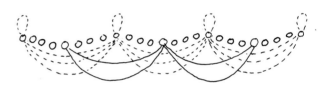

Figure 4

Black and White Cake

For a strikingly graphic cake when pastels are not appropriate, such as a bar mitzvah or a sophisticated anniversary, this creation can be a dramatic solution. Since black icing is not very appetizing, the decorations are made primarily from different forms of licorice.

Serves 115

Cakes:

12-inch round, 3 inches high (2 layers)
10-inch round, 3 inches high (2 layers)
8-inch round, 3 inches high (2 layers)
6-inch round, 4 inches high (2 layers)

1 recipe royal icing
waxed paper
3 recipes pure white basic buttercream icing
black licorice shoestrings, sticks, and buttons
small black candy balls
unsweetened cocoa powder
16-inch round foam board, 3 layers thick
14-inch, 12-inch, 10-inch, 8-inch, and 6-inch
    round foam boards
black food coloring
cloth-covered wire
tips #2, #6, #44, #127D

In advance:

Cover the 16-inch board with thinned white royal icing. Let it dry for twenty-four hours. Place the board on a piece of waxed paper that extends out all around the board. Pipe royal icing dots around the edge of the board, using the #6 tip, and insert black candies into the icing. Let this dry for twenty-four hours. When the icing is dry, glue the 14-inch board to the bottom of the 16-inch board.

To decorate the cake:

Bake all cakes and let them cool. Add filling between the layers. Place each tier on a foam board and cover with white buttercream. Stack the tiers according to directions for tiered cakes (pages 26–28). Measure the height of the 6-inch and 10-inch tiers and cut licorice sticks to those heights. Pipe thin vertical lines of buttercream with the #2 tip and attach the licorice sticks to the sides of these tiers. Space licorice sticks evenly, about 1 inch apart, all around the two tiers.

For the remaining two tiers, pipe small dots of icing and attach the licorice buttons. Place the buttons in a checkerboard formation.

To make the ruffles at the base of the tiers, use the #127D tip and white buttercream. Since this is a large tip, a coupler is not used. Place the tip directly into the pastry bag. Hold the wide end of the tip against the cake, with the opening facing down. Move the tip up and down slightly as you apply pressure to the bag (Figure 1). Pipe a double row of ruffles around

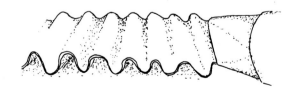

Figure 1

the base of the 12-inch tier and a single row around the other layers.

Black icing is used only to make the small polka dots and stripes on the ruffles. Add unsweetened cocoa powder to ¾ cup of buttercream. Mix in a small amount of black food coloring until the icing is a dark gray. The icing will get darker as it sets, so only a small amount of black is needed. Pipe small dots onto the ruffles at the base of the 10-inch and 6-inch tiers with the #2 tip.

Pipe a double row of black stripes on the other ruffles, using the #44 tip.

To make the bow on the top, gather loops of licorice strings about 4 inches long. Gather into a large cluster and tie them together with a long piece of cloth-covered wire. Twist the wire tightly around the end of the loops. Cut off the excess licorice close to the wire. Insert into the top of the cake and gently spread the loops apart.

Part IV

Advanced Cakes

Easy Chair

This cake was created after I participated in a show called "Edible Architecture/Delicious Designs," for which I made a cake that looked like a bed. I decided to try my hand at other types of furniture. Perfect for a retirement or a house warming party, this cake will make everyone sit up and take notice.

Serves 15

3 8-inch square cakes, 2 inches high
1 recipe royal icing
waxed paper
11x15-inch foam board, 2 layers thick
3½-inch-wide tart pan sugar mold
2½-inch-wide tart pan sugar mold
¼-inch wooden dowels
power drill with ¼-inch bit
small paintbrush
gold paint
gold edible powder
lemon extract
1 recipe gum paste to make the book (optional)
1 recipe buttercream icing
1 recipe rolled fondant
8-inch square foam board
yellow, brown, orange, and blue paste food
        coloring
tips #4, #15, #44

In advance:

Make the rug first. Cut the 11x15-inch double-thickness piece of foam board into an oval (Figure 1). Place the oval on top of a piece of waxed paper that is larger than the oval, using a dab of icing to hold it in place. Tint 1

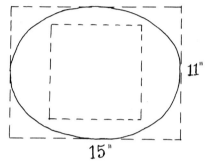

Figure 1

cup of royal icing straw color by mixing yellow and brown. With the #15 tip, start piping shells around the outside edge of the oval, to cover the edge of the board, and continue making concentric ovals until the entire board is covered. Set this aside to dry for twenty-four hours.

To make the lamp, make the two sugar molds (see pages 9–10) and let them dry for at least two days. Cut a dowel to measure 7½ inches long. Paint the dowel with gold paint. Using a power drill, drill a ¼-inch hole halfway through the center of each mold, drilling from the wide end of the large mold and through the narrow end of the smaller mold. Pipe a small amount of royal icing into the hole of the smaller sugar mold and insert the gold dowel into the hole. Let this dry for twenty-four hours.

When the icing in the first sugar mold has dried, pipe a little royal icing into the hole of the larger sugar mold and place on top of the gold dowel. Let it dry for twenty-four hours.

Paint the bottom sugar mold with gold pow-

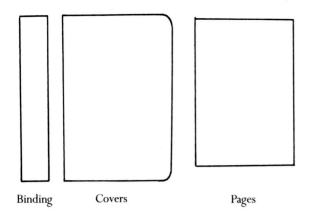

Binding   Covers   Pages

Figure 2

Figure 3

der mixed with a few drops of lemon extract.

To make the book, make the gum paste and let it set for twenty-four hours at room temperature. Using the patterns provided, cut the pieces to form the book (Figure 2). (See directions for gum paste on page 9.) The gum paste covers and binding edge should be about ⅛ inch thick. The pages should be rolled as thin as possible and two of the pages should be dried on a curved surface, such as a cardboard tube from a paper towel roll. Cut two pieces for the cover of the book and eight pages. Cut one piece for the binding. Let these pieces dry for at least twenty-four hours.

When the pieces for the book have dried, paint the pieces that make up the cover and binding of the book with brown coloring mixed with a little lemon extract. Let these pieces dry for a few hours.

To construct the book, pipe a line of royal icing down the center of the binding piece. Place the straight edges of both covers in the icing. Pipe another line of icing down the center of the book, and insert the pages into the wet icing. Place some wadded Kleenex between the pages to allow them to dry in a slightly separated position. Let the book dry for twenty-four hours (Figure 3).

Make the rolled fondant and tint it a pale blue. Let it set for twenty-four hours, wrapped in plastic and sealed in an airtight container.

To decorate the cake:

Bake all of the cakes and let them cool. Place the bottom 8-inch square on the 8-inch board with a dab of icing. Spread filling on top of this layer and set the next 8-inch layer on top. Cut out a piece of the second layer that measures 5 inches across the front, 4 inches toward the back, and is 2 inches deep (Figure 4).

Cut the remaining 8-inch layer in half. Spread a layer of filling on the area behind the cut-out section on the chair. Place one half of the 8-inch layer on the back section of the

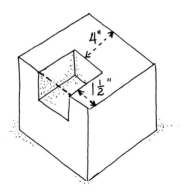

Figure 4

chair. Add filling to the top of the piece you just added and place the other half of the 8-inch square on top. To give the back of the chair support, insert two dowels or plastic straws into the back of the cake, and cut to the height of the chair (Figure 5).

Using a serrated knife, trim the cake to round off all of the edges (Figure 6). Cover the entire cake with buttercream.

Cover the cake with blue rolled fondant, easing the fondant into all of the corners of the cake. It will be easier to cover the cake if the fondant is put on in sections. Measure the back of the cake from the seat, over the back to the floor. Cut a piece of blue fondant and drape the piece onto the back. Smooth the icing over the cake and make a seam along the back sides. Measure the width of the chair from the bottom of the left side, up and over the arm, across the seat, and down the right side. Measure the seat from the first piece of fondant to the floor. Cut the fondant to this size, and drape it over the cake, easing it into the rounded areas. Smooth the icing with your hands.

Place a dab of buttercream on the center of the rug and place the cake on top.

Cut out eight ½-inch circles of fondant with the back of a decorating tip and set these aside. These will form the buttons.

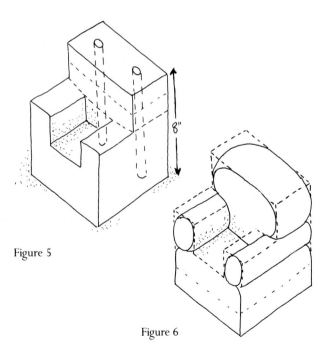

Figure 5

Figure 6

The ruffles for the bottom of the chair are made in three pieces. Roll out a piece of fondant and cut a strip 2 inches wide and about 10 inches long. Fold the fondant strip to form a ruffle (Figure 7). Measure the side of the cake.

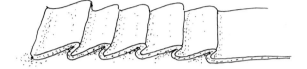

Figure 7

Cut the strip to fit the side of the cake. Moisten the side of the cake where the ruffle will go with a small paintbrush and a little water. Attach the top of the ruffle to the side of the cake. Repeat on the other side of the cake. Make the third ruffle for the front of the cake and attach, tucking the ends of the side ruffles under the front one.

Take a sharpened wooden dowel and press into the fondant in a dot formation along the top of the ruffles.

Using the #44 tip, pipe yellow royal icing vertical stripes, starting at the top of the cake and running down to the front of the seat. Stop piping at the top of the ruffle. Then continue the line from the top of the ruffle to the floor. Space the stripes evenly, about 1 inch apart.

The stripes for the arms of the chair are piped perpendicular to the first set of stripes. Start at the inside of the seat and pipe over the arm and down to the top of the ruffle. Then continue the stripe on the ruffle to the floor.

Using the #4 tip, pipe orange royal icing stripes on either side of the yellow stripes.

Pipe a dot of icing on the back of each of the buttons and attach six to the chair above the seat, in a "V" formation. Attach the two remaining buttons to the front of each arm.

Place the book on the seat of the chair and the lamp next to it, and you have a little home "sweet" home.

Sweet Heart

This cake was created for Gene Moore for a window of Tiffany & Company in New York. It's perfect for Valentine's Day or a wedding shower.

Serves 25

12-inch heart cake, 4 inches high (2 layers)
20 assorted toothpick roses, lilies, petunias, carnations, and daisies in pink, red, white, and lilac (pages 15–19)
10 clusters of baby's breath (page 19)
2 recipes gum paste
round toothpicks
1 egg white
1 recipe royal icing
waxed paper
2 recipes rolled fondant
1 recipe buttercream icing
small heart-shaped gum paste cutter
16-inch heart-shaped board, covered in red foil (use the cake pan as a guide)
ruler
serrated pattern tracing wheel
small paintbrush
red and green paste food coloring
tips #2, #4, #13, #68

In advance:

Make all of the flowers and allow them to dry for at least twenty-four hours.

Make the gum paste. Set aside one recipe of gum paste, which will be used to make the ruffle. Divide the other recipe of gum paste into three equal portions. Leave one portion white and tint the other two portions red and pink.

Place all of the paste in plastic bags and place in an airtight container. Let them set for twenty-four hours at room temperature.

After the gum paste has set, make four toothpick loops in each color, as described in the section on gum paste bows (pages 22–23). Make three ribbons on toothpicks in each color (page 23). Make a few extra of each in case of breakage. Let these dry for at least twenty-four hours. The remaining paste will be used for the streamers, which will be applied directly onto the cake.

Make the hearts for the lace border on waxed paper with white royal icing, using the #1 tip and following the pattern provided (Figure 1). You will need about forty of these, but make extra in case of breakage. Set aside to dry overnight.

Figure 1

Make two batches of rolled fondant and divide one of the batches in half. One of these halves will remain white for the ruffle. Tint the other one and one-half batches of the fondant a pale pink. Let all of the fondant rest for twenty-four hours, wrapped in plastic and placed in an airtight container at room temperature.

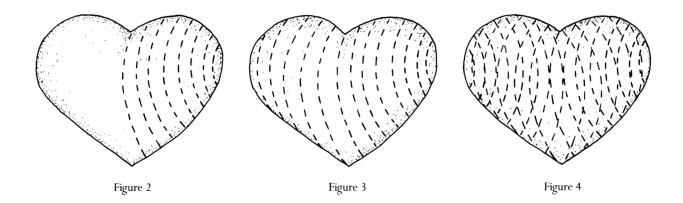

Figure 2   Figure 3   Figure 4

To decorate the cake:

Bake the cakes and cool. Place the bottom layer on the foil-covered base with a dab of buttercream. Add filling and place the second layer on top. Round all the edges of the cake by cutting with a serrated knife.

Coat the cake with thinned buttercream icing to smooth the surface. Ice again with more buttercream after the first coat has set. Cover the cake with the pink rolled fondant, using a pizza cutter or sharp knife to trim the excess from the bottom of the cake.

To mark the cake for the quilt lines, take a toothpick and make small marks ¾ inch up from the bottom edge of the cake. Make marks 1 inch apart going all around the cake, beginning at the tip of the heart and marking from the left and right. This is where your quilt lines will start.

With the tracing wheel, emboss curved lines in the fondant, beginning in the front of the cake and ending in the back (Figure 2). Make all of the lines curving to the left first (Figure 3). Then make crossed lines curving to the right (Figure 4).

To make the 7-inch white heart for the center of the cake, draw a 7-inch circle on a piece of paper and fold the paper in half. Cut out half of a heart with the paper folded, so that when you open the paper you will have a complete heart (Figures 5 and 6). Roll out a very thin piece of white fondant and place the pattern on top of it. Using the pattern as a template, cut out the heart shape in the fondant. Slide both hands under the fondant heart and place it in the center of the cake. Smooth it down with your hands.

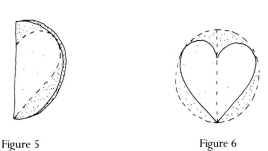

Figure 5   Figure 6

Using the small, heart-shaped cutter, emboss hearts all around the inside edge of the white heart. Emboss dots with a toothpick around the small hearts.

To make the ruffle edge, measure the bottom edge of the cake with a tape measure and divide the length in half. Knead together the remaining white fondant and the white gum paste until fully blended. Roll out the fondant/gum paste mixture on a cornstarch-dusted pastry cloth or a smooth, clean surface. Roll out to ¹⁄₁₆-inch thickness and cut two strips 2 inches wide by the length of the half heart measure, using a sharp knife and ruler to cut the strip straight.

Using the end of a paintbrush, roll the brush back and forth along one edge of the strip (Figure 7). You will see that the strip will begin to ruffle.

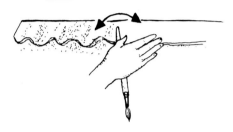

Figure 7

To attach the ruffle to the cake, wet a small paintbrush with water and run along the edge of the cake. Start attaching the ruffle to the moistened edge at the front of the cake and press it along the edge to the middle of the back of the cake. Make the second ruffle and place it along the other edge. Since ruffling tends to make the strip longer, cut off any extra length at the back of the cake. Where the two ruffles meet, fold down the ends and gently press together with your fingers.

If the ruffles start to droop, place small balls of Kleenex or paper toweling under the ruffles to hold them up until they set.

If you wish, you may add a second ruffle above the first one, repeating the same procedure as for the first ruffle.

Pipe a thin shell border along the edge of the ruffle where it meets the cake, with royal icing and the #13 tip. After the second ruffle has set for half an hour, pipe a royal icing loop edge along the outer edge of the ruffle, using a #2 tip. Pipe drop strings at the centers of each of the shells (Figure 8).

With the #4 tip, pipe small hearts of red royal icing at the intersections of all of the quilt lines (Figures 9 and 10).

Pipe a few dots with white royal icing and the #2 tip along the edge of the white heart. Carefully slide a metal spatula under the small white piped hearts to loosen them from the waxed paper. Attach the hearts to the beads of icing along the border of the white heart, while the icing is wet.

Roll out the remaining colored gum paste and cut ten thin strips about 5 inches long and ⅜ inch wide. Notch one end of the ribbon and attach the other end to the inside of the white heart, about 2 inches from the edge, using a little water to stick the ribbon on the fondant. Lay each ribbon down the front of the cake so they have a curved, ribbon-like shape. Press the end of the ribbon gently in place.

Insert the flowers into the center of the cake, within the white heart. With the #68 tip, pipe leaves in green buttercream around the base of each flower after the flower has been inserted into the cake.

Insert the ten gum paste loops and ribbons in the top of the white heart, piping more green leaves around their bases.

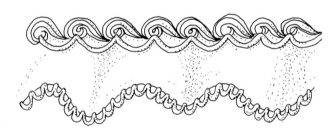

Figure 8

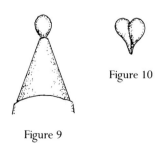

Figure 9

Figure 10

Chocolate Teddy Bear

This cake was actually made for a man who collected teddy bears. But the cheerful little bear will make any child's birthday party a memorable occasion.

Serves 35

Cakes:

3 halves of a 6-inch ball
6-inch round, 3 inches high (2 layers)
6-inch square, 2 inches high

1 recipe rolled fondant
2 recipes basic buttercream icing
½ cup unsweetened cocoa powder
2 wafer cookies
3 chocolate discs, 1 inch wide
foam board
12-inch square foam board, 3 layers thick
3 ¼-inch wooden dowels, each 12 inches long
    with one end sharpened
2 black bead candies
red and blue paste food coloring
tips #3, #5, #48, #233

In advance:

Make the fondant, wrap it in plastic, place it in an airtight container, and let it set for twenty-four hours at room temperature.

To decorate the cake:

Bake all of the cakes and let them cool. Cover the 12-inch base with decorative paper or foil.

Cut a piece of foam board into a 6-inch round with two extensions that measure 2 inches wide by 3 inches long, from the edge of the circle. The extensions should be 1½ inches apart at the edge of the circle and 4 inches apart at their ends. Round off the ends of the two extending pieces. This will be the support for the arms (Figure 1). Insert three dowels into the board to make three holes.

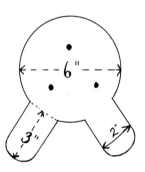

Figure 1

Place one of the 6-inch round layers on the covered 12-inch board, using a little buttercream to hold it in place. Add filling and then the second layer. Cover the top of the cake with buttercream.

Place the foam board with the two extensions on top of the bottom layers. Insert the sharpened ends of the 12-inch wooden dowels through the pre-made holes, through the cake and into the base (Figure 2).

Cut 1 inch off the rounded half of one of the 6-inch ball halves to make a flat area. Place the half ball, wide edge down, onto the top of the foam board, through the dowels. Add buttercream on top of this layer (Figure 3).

113

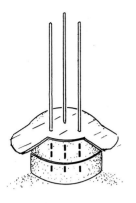

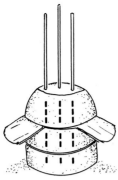

Figure 2   Figure 3

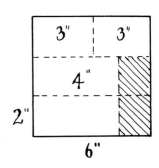

Figure 5

Cut off the top of another half ball and place it cut side down over the first half ball, through the dowels. Add filling and place the top ball, round side up, on this layer. Cut off the tops of the dowels (Figure 4).

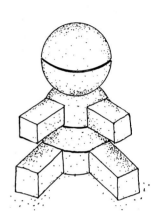

Figure 6   Figure 7

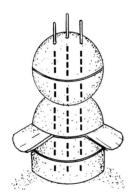

Figure 4

To make the eye and nose area on the head of the bear, cut a 3-inch circle around the front, bottom half of the head (Figure 8). Cut down around the 3-inch circle about 1 inch in toward the center of the cake (Figure 9). Remove the wedge from the face (Figure 10).

Cover the upper area of the bear's body with white buttercream icing. Roll out the fondant

Cut the 6-inch square cake into five pieces, as illustrated (Figure 5). Attach two 4-inch-long pieces of cake to the bottom of the cake for the legs. Use icing to glue the legs to the body and the base (Figure 6).

Attach the two 3-inch pieces of cake to each of the extensions of foam board with icing (Figure 7).

Using a serrated knife, round off the arms and legs.

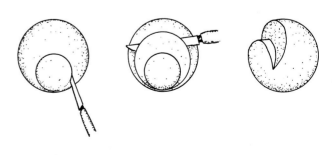

Figure 8   Figure 9   Figure 10

and attach a piece to the back of the bear for the T-shirt.

Roll out another piece of fondant and attach to the front of the bear. Ease the fondant into the curves of the arms and cut off the excess fondant.

Place two of the wafer cookies into the cake at the top of the head for the ears. Spread chocolate buttercream (add unsweetened cocoa powder to the remaining buttercream, to make it brown; reserve ¾ cup for the red and blue piping) on the fronts of the ears, the ends of the feet, and around the nose area.

Pipe chocolate fur all over the bear with the #233 tip, using the photograph as a guide. Outline the shirt with red icing, using the #48 tip. Pipe the child's name on the front of the shirt with blue buttercream, using the #5 tip.

Place the two chocolate candy discs on the head for the eyes. Cut the third chocolate candy disc into a triangular shape and place it on the end of the nose (Figure 11). Use a dab of buttercream to hold the discs in place. Pipe a line of chocolate icing with the #5 tip for the mouth, and add black candy beads in the centers of the eyes (Figure 12).

Figure 11

Figure 12

4th of July Cake Mobile

What child could resist a cake that is covered with candy? The idea for this cake developed after I made a sculpture that looked like a wedding cake on wheels for a toy show. This cake will make any child's eyes light up with joy. (A lightweight cake is recommended.)

Serves 35

Cakes:

10-inch square, 3½ inches high (2 layers)
8-inch square, 2 inches high

1 recipe royal icing
waxed paper
white cloth-covered wires
orange and blue edible glitter
multicolored sprinkles
vodka
4-inch Styrofoam cube
7x10-inch foam board, 2 layers thick

2 wooden dowels, ½ inch thick and 12 inches long
white glue
8 large multicolored lollipops, of equal size
power drill with ½-inch bit
3 recipes pure white basic buttercream icing
4x8-inch piece of foam board
plastic drinking straws
silver dragees
12 multicolored candy sticks
18 small lollipops
1 spherical sucker
12-inch length of red licorice whip
assorted candies: red hearts, snowcaps,
    multicolored mints, pastel licorice candies,
    nonpareils, candy beads
blue, orange, yellow, and red paste food coloring
tips #2, #17, #21

In advance:

Make six run-in sugar stars on wires with the #2 tip, using the patterns shown (Figure 1).

Figure 1

(See directions for run-in sugar on page 8.) Sprinkle the stars with colored sprinkles or colored glitter while the icing is wet. When the icing is dry, turn the stars over and fill in with another layer of run-in sugar and decorate as the first side. Let the stars dry for twenty-four hours.

To make the three corkscrew wires for the top, soak three white wires in separate batches of red, blue, and orange food coloring with a little vodka added. Place the wires on a paper towel to dry. When the wires are dry, twist a colored wire around a white wire and then wrap the two wires around a pencil. Repeat with all the colored wires.

Make a three-sided pyramid from the 4-inch cube of Styrofoam. Using a serrated knife, cut the cube diagonally to measure 3½ inches on the two right-angle sides and 5 inches along the diagonal (Figure 2). Set aside the larger section. Next, find the center of the top of the smaller piece of Styrofoam. Slice off the edges diagonally from the center to the base to form a pyramid (Figure 3). Sand the cut sides smooth with the other piece of Styrofoam.

To decorate the pyramid, first adhere the base of the pyramid to a piece of waxed paper with a dab of royal icing. While icing the pyramid, leave a small space at the top un-iced to enable easy insertion of the wired stars. The un-iced section can be finished after the stars are in place.

Ice one side of the pyramid with white royal icing and, while it is still wet, cover it with multicolored sprinkles. Ice another side of the pyramid with yellow royal icing and attach pink, blue, and yellow mint candies in a polka-dot pattern. Ice the third side with vertical lines of blue royal icing piped with the #17 tip. Decorate with white mint candies and silver dragees.

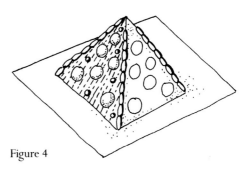

Figure 4

Finish the diagonal edges of the pyramid with a line of piped white royal icing shells made with the #17 tip. Pipe another line of shells on either side of the first piped line. Place pastel licorice candies in the icing in a line along the edges (Figure 4). Set the pyramid aside to dry for at least twenty-four hours.

To prepare the wheels, first cut off the sticks of the large lollipops with a small saw or serrated knife, being careful not to break the lollipop. Sand the rough end of the stick so that the remaining stick is flush with the lollipop. Trace the outline of one of the lollipops on a piece of paper. Find the center of the circle by folding the paper in quarters. Place the piece of paper over the lollipop and drill a ½-inch hole

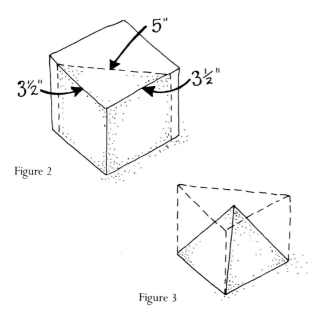

Figure 2

Figure 3

into the lollipop through the center of the piece of paper. Repeat this procedure on all of the lollipops. Check to make sure that a ½-inch dowel fits snugly into the holes drilled. If the dowel doesn't fit, enlarge the hole in the lollipop slightly with the drill. Glue four sets of two lollipops together with royal icing, making sure that the sticks inside each lollipop line up with each other on each set of two lollipops. This will give each wheel added strength when the cake is set on the wheels. Set aside to dry overnight.

Glue the two ½-inch dowels to the bottom of the double-thickness 7x10-inch foam board, 1½ inches in from each end (Figure 5). Let the glue dry overnight. Make a pencil mark on each dowel, ½ inch out from the edge of the board (Figure 6). Measure the depth of one of the sets of two lollipops. Make a mark on the dowel that is the same as this measurement, measuring from the ½-inch mark and extending out toward the end of the dowel (Figure 7). Cut the dowel with a small saw at the outermost pencil mark.

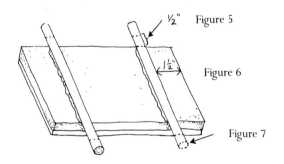

Figure 5

Figure 6

Figure 7

To construct the cake:

Bake the cakes and let them cool. Cut the 10-inch layers to measure 7 inches by 10 inches. Stack the 10-inch layers, adding filling in between. Place the cake on the 7x10-inch foam board (with the dowels facing down), attaching it with a dab of buttercream. Cut one end of

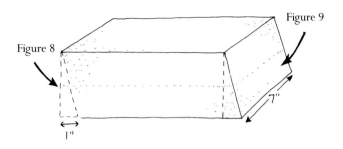

Figure 8

Figure 9

the cake diagonally, from the top of the cake, in 1 inch (Figure 8) and attach the cut end to the other uncut end with buttercream (Figure 9). Place the cake 1 inch from one edge of the board. The cut piece will fill in this area when it is added. Cover the cake with thinned white buttercream. Insert plastic straws as described in the section on tiered cakes using the 4x8-inch foam board as a guide as to where to place the straws (pages 26–28).

Cut the 8-inch square cake in half. Place one half on the 4 inch by 8 inch foam board and attach it with a dab of buttercream. Add filling and place the second half on top of the first half. Cut off 1 inch diagonally on one end of the cake, starting at the division of the two layers (Figure 10). Then cut diagonally on the top, 1 inch from the right end of the cake and down to the division of the two layers (Figure 11). Make a third diagonal cut starting at the 1-inch cut on the top, down to the bottom of the cake (Figure 12). Cover the 8-inch cake with a thin layer of buttercream. Place the 8-inch layer on top of the 10-inch bottom layer,

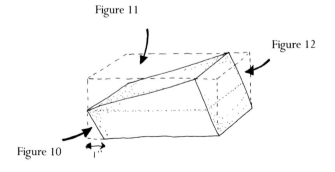

Figure 11

Figure 12

Figure 10

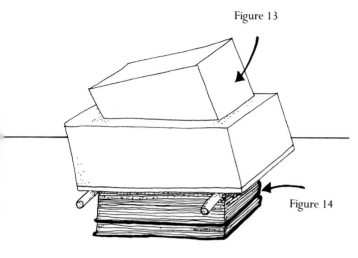

Figure 13

Figure 14

securing it with a dab of buttercream (Figure 13).

Place the entire cake on a raised surface (such as a stack of books) so that the cake will be higher than the height of the wheels (Figure 14).

To decorate the bottom tier, pipe vertical lines with white buttercream using the #17 tip up one side of the cake. Attach a small lollipop right side up, then the next one upside down, and so on, spacing the lollipops evenly in the icing. Add silver dragees in between the lollipops. Continue all around the bottom tier.

To decorate the second tier, pipe a vertical line of blue buttercream with the #17 tip up the corner of the cake. Cut a candy stick, using snippers, to the height of the tier. Attach the candy stick to the buttercream. Attach candy sticks about 1 inch apart, all around the side of the tier, first cutting the candy to the correct height and then piping a line of buttercream to

hold the candy in place. Fill in the spaces between the candy sticks with zigzag lines of blue buttercream.

Cover the top of the 10-inch layer with pink stars, using the #17 tip. Place snowcaps randomly among the stars.

Place the top pyramid on a piece of waxed paper the same size as the base of the pyramid, using a dab of buttercream to hold it in place. Insert the stars and colored wires into the top of the pyramid. Fill in any bare spots at the top of the pyramid with white buttercream. Attach the pyramid to the top of the second tier with buttercream.

Cover the top of the second tier with white buttercream stars, using the #17 tip, and place red hearts and dragees all around. With the #21 tip, pipe yellow shell borders onto all of the edges of the bottom tier. Pipe white shell borders onto the top edge of the second tier.

To add the wheels, pipe some royal icing onto the ends of the ½-inch dowels and inside the drilled holes in the lollipops. Insert the wheels onto the dowels. Arrange the wheels so that the part of the wheel resting on the table is on the end of the lollipop stick. This is very important, because the stick adds strength to the wheel. Glue a nonpareil to the center of each wheel with a dab of royal icing and place colored candy beads all around the nonpareils. Let the royal icing set for twenty-four hours.

When ready to serve, remove the cake from the stack of books and place the cake on the table. Insert the licorice whip into the front of the cake. Cut off the end of the licorice so that the end is open and insert the stick of the spherical sucker into the licorice.

Multicolored Bow Cake

I designed this cake for a party given by a ribbon manufacturer. It's perfect for a birthday party or, if made in all white, it can be used as a wedding cake.

Serves 75

Cakes:

12-inch round, 2 inches high
8-inch round, 3 inches high
5-inch round, 3 inches high

4 recipes gum paste
round toothpicks
1 egg white
1 recipe yellow royal icing
waxed paper
16-inch round foam board, 3 layers thick
14-inch round foam board
3-inch Styrofoam ball, cut in half
2 recipes buttercream icing
¼-inch wooden dowels or plastic drinking straws
5-inch, 8-inch, and 12-inch round foam boards
yellow, pink, red, green, blue, purple, and peach
    paste food coloring
tips #3 and #19

In advance:

Make all of the gum paste. Divide all of the paste into seven equal portions. Tint each portion a different color: red, green, pink, purple, blue, peach, and yellow. Place each portion in a tightly sealed plastic bag and place the bags in an airtight container. Let them set for twenty-four hours at room temperature.

Cover the 16-inch triple-layer foam board with thinned yellow royal icing, as described in the section on cake boards (pages 25–26). When they are completely dry, place the board on a sheet of waxed paper that is larger than the board. Pipe a #19 shell border all around the edge of the board with stiff yellow royal icing. Let the board dry for twenty-four hours. When it is dry, remove the waxed paper and glue the 14-inch foam board underneath the base.

Make loops and ribbons with all of the gum paste. You will need ninety loops and sixty ribbons. These are all made on toothpicks, as described in the section on gum paste ribbons and bows (pages 22–23). Allow these to dry thoroughly for at least two days.

To make the top decoration, cut a 3-inch Styrofoam ball in half and attach to a piece of waxed paper with a dab of royal icing. Begin inserting the toothpick ends of the dried ribbons and loops into the ball, starting at the top and working down on all sides of the ball. For every four loops, add two ribbons. When you have placed about six loops and ribbons in the ball, pipe some yellow royal icing onto the ball around the bases of the loops and ribbons, using the #19 tip. This will hold them in place. Continue adding loops and ribbons and piping royal icing onto the ball until the entire ball is covered. Let this dry for twenty-four hours.

To decorate the cake:

Bake all of the cakes and let them cool completely. Place the bottom tier on the 12-inch board and the 5-inch and 8-inch tiers on the

other boards. Add filling between the layers and ice smooth with yellow buttercream. Insert dowels or plastic straws into the 12-inch and 8-inch tiers. Stack the cakes, as described in the section on tiered cakes (pages 26–28). Pipe a shell border around the base of each tier with the #19 tip and yellow buttercream.

Using the #3 tip, pipe polka-dots all around the cake with yellow buttercream.

If the cake is to have candles, decide where you want to place the candles. Place the candles around the cake, evenly spaced. The clusters of bows and ribbons will be placed between the candles.

Next, insert the remaining loops and ribbons in the cake, between the candles. Place all of the ribbons and loops on the cake.

The finishing touch is to place the top decoration on the cake. Remove the top decoration from the waxed paper. Cut a circle of waxed paper the same size as the base of the Styrofoam ball. Place the Styrofoam ball on the circle, secured with a dab of buttercream, and place the top decoration on the cake with a dab of buttercream to hold it in place.

Golden Jubilee

I made this cake for my parents' fiftieth wedding anniversary. The hardest part was getting it from New York to San Francisco on an airplane! Each layer was packed separately in a box, and, luckily, since the plane was almost empty because of the earthquake a week before, there was plenty of storage space.

The bride and groom were reproduced from my parents' original wedding picture and two of the layers were covered with 22-karat gold leaf, which is edible. The end result is a beautiful cake that should provide the bride and groom with another fifty years' worth of memories.

Serves 100

Cakes:

half of a 6-inch ball
6-inch round, 3 inches high (2 layers)
7-inch round, 1 inch high
10-inch round, 4 inches high (2 layers)
12-inch round, 2 inches high

3 recipes royal icing
waxed paper
edible gold powder
lemon extract
small and medium-sized soft paintbrushes
6 cupid sugar molds, 3 facing left and 3 facing right (the molds can be found in cake-decorating stores)
3-inch sugar mold from a scalloped tart pan
1-inch Styrofoam ball

gold dragees
7 7-inch columns
2 8-inch separator plates
gold enamel spray paint
white glue
16-inch round foam board base, three layers thick
14-inch round foam board
X-acto knife
¼-inch wooden dowels
2 recipes buttercream icing
4 recipes rolled fondant
12-inch, 10-inch, and 6-inch round foam boards
pink iridescent powder
pastry brush
1 packet 22-karat gold leaf (found in art supply stores)
tips #2, #3, #14, #17, #65

In advance:

Draw eight 2-inch circles on a piece of paper. Place waxed paper on top of the circles and tape down on a flat surface. Pipe white run-in sugar with the #2 tip onto the waxed paper to fill in the circles (see page 8). Let them set for a few hours. Then, with stiff white royal icing and the #3 tip, pipe the number 50 on each disc. Then pipe a shell border around each disc, using the #14 tip. Let these dry at least twenty-four hours. When the discs are completely dry, paint them with about ¼ teaspoon of gold powder mixed with a few drops of lemon extract. The lemon extract rapidly evaporates, so you will probably have to keep adding more as you work.

Make all of the sugar molds (see pages 9–10). Before the tart pan mold has completely dried, hollow out the inside and fit a 1-inch Styrofoam ball into the top of the mold. Let all of the molds dry completely, at least twenty-four hours.

Pipe some royal icing at the feet of two of the left-facing cupids and set the center of a right-facing cupid on top of each to glue them together (Figure 1). Let them dry completely. When they are dry, paint all of the cupids with the gold powder and lemon extract mixture.

Figure 1

Pipe a shell border with royal icing using the #14 tip around the top edge of the tart sugar mold and insert a gold dragee at each intersection of the scallops. When the icing has dried, paint the entire mold, except for the Styrofoam ball, with gold powder and lemon extract. Carefully insert the feet of one of the double cupids into the top of the Styrofoam ball and glue it in place with a little royal icing. Pipe green leaves with royal icing, using the #65 tip, all around the ball and finish with randomly placed pale pink dots, using the #3 tip.

Spray-paint the columns and the pegged side of one of the separator plates with gold paint. When dry, pipe a green royal icing spiral along the entire height of each column, using the

#14 tip. With a #65 tip and green icing, pipe leaves along each spiral. Then pipe pink dots along the spirals, using the #3 tip. (Note: The icing on the painted areas should not be eaten.)

Place four of the columns in the pegs on the bottom of the gold separator plate. Glue the other three columns in place with royal icing between the four columns. Leave a space in the front for the bride and groom.

Pipe a royal icing border around the scalloped edge of the bottom separator plate with the #14 tip. Place a gold dragee at the intersections of all the scallops. When the icing has dried, paint with gold powder and lemon extract.

To make the base for the cake, cover the 16-inch foam board with thinned white royal icing. Place the board on a sheet of waxed paper that is larger than the board. Using the #14 tip, pipe a royal icing border around the sides of the base, using a vertical zigzag motion to cover the entire edge. When completely dry, paint the top and sides of the board with gold powder and lemon extract. Remove the board from the waxed paper and glue the 14-inch board underneath it with white glue.

If you are going to use an old wedding picture for the bride and groom, make a photocopy of the original photograph and glue it onto a piece of foam board. Carefully cut around the figures with a sharp X-acto knife. Glue a triangle of foam board to the back of the cut-out figures to make a stand. Carefully paint the photocopy with watercolors to give them a realistic appearance.

Make all of the rolled fondant and tint it a pale pink. Let it set for twenty-four hours at room temperature wrapped in plastic and placed in an airtight container.

To assemble the cake:

Bake all of the cakes and let them cool. Place the 12-inch, 10-inch, and 6-inch cakes on their separator boards, and place the 7-inch layer on the 8-inch separator plate. The 6-inch half ball is placed on top of the 6-inch round layers. Add filling to the tiers and ice the tops and sides with buttercream. Cover all of the tiers with fondant. Add dowels to all but the top tier, as described in the section on tiered cakes (pages 26–28).

Lightly dust the 10-inch and 6-inch tiers with pink iridescent powder, using a medium-sized paintbrush.

To apply the gold leaf to the bottom tier, dip a clean pastry brush in water and shake off the excess. Brush the surface of the fondant lightly, until the fondant is sticky. Press a sheet of gold leaf against the surface of the fondant and carefully remove the paper backing. Use a small dry brush to tap down any of the gold that does not adhere immediately. Be careful not to rub the gold too much or it will start to dissolve. Continue adding gold leaf to the surface of the 12-inch tier until it is covered up to 1 inch over the top edge. The top of the cake will not be covered with gold, since the 10-inch tier will be placed on it.

If there are any bare spots that the gold leaf does not cover, brush the area carefully with a small damp brush, and reapply a small piece of gold to that area. The gold will adhere only to an area that is sticky.

Next, place the 10-inch tier on top of the 12-inch tier. Place the separator plate with the columns on top.

Cover the 7-inch tier with gold leaf, up to ¼ inch over the top.

Place the 6-inch tier on top of the 7-inch layer. Pipe a little royal icing onto the tops of the three columns that will not be in a peg. Place the top separator plate, with the 7-inch and 6-inch tiers, on top of the columns, fitting the four top pegs into the four corresponding columns.

To decorate the cake, the columns and sepa-

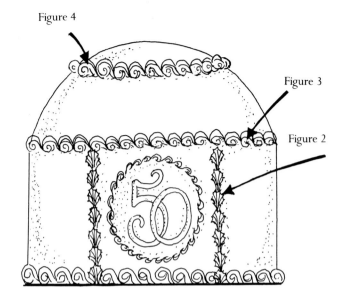

Figure 4

Figure 3

Figure 2

rator plates can be used as a guide as to where to place your decorations. Start with the run-in sugar discs and glue the first one with royal icing on the 6-inch tier, about ½ inch from the top of the 7-inch layer. Center the first disc above the area between the columns where the bride and groom will be placed. Center all of the other discs above a column, making sure that they are evenly spaced.

With royal icing and the #14 tip, pipe a vertical line of shells between the discs from the base of the 6-inch tier to about ¼ inch above the discs (Figure 2). Pipe a horizontal line of shells ¼ inch above the discs, and another about 2 inches from the top of the dome (Figures 3 and 4). Pipe a shell border around the base of the 6-inch tier, and outline the scalloped edge of the top separator plate.

Divide the top edge of the 10-inch tier in quarters with a toothpick for placement of the garlands. Place marks on the top edge of the tier in line with the front two columns, and another set of marks about 1 inch up from the base, centered between the columns. Continue around the cake, marking at the base of the first and third columns, and at the base of the

Figure 5

third and fifth columns. Pipe four reverse shell garlands with the #14 tip and royal icing around the 10-inch tier (Figure 5).

Glue the two single cupids on the left and right side of the 10-inch tier with royal icing, just under the top of the garland. Glue one set of two cupids that have been glued together in the center of the garland in the front of the cake.

Pipe shells around the base of the 10-inch and 12-inch tiers with the #17 tip and royal icing.

Let all of the royal icing shells on the cake dry for two hours. Then paint them with gold powder mixed with lemon extract, using a small brush. Be careful not to disturb the shells, for they will not yet be totally dry.

Starting at the top of the cake and working down, pipe pale green royal icing leaves with a #65 tip. Pipe leaves around the bottom of the first shell line in Figure 4, piping one leaf at each intersection of all the shells. Pipe leaves at the top of the horizontal line in Figure 3 in the same manner. Pipe two leaves at the top of each of the discs, and at the top and bottom of each vertical line in Figure 2, the top ones facing down and the bottom ones facing up.

Pipe leaves at the base of all of the tiers, including the bottom of the separator plates. Pipe vertical leaves around the bases of the 7-inch, 10-inch, and 12-inch tiers.

Pipe leaves at the intersections of the shells in the garlands, alternating the leaves so that one points up, the next one down, and so on.

Pipe a cluster of leaves at the top of each garland and underneath the cupids, curving the leaves to the left and right. Pipe another cluster of leaves in the same manner on the 12-inch tier, underneath the left and right cupids.

Mix some pale pink royal icing and, using the #3 tip, pipe clusters of dots around all of the gold shells and borders.

Finally, glue the top sugar mold in place with royal icing and pipe a leaf and dot border all around the base of the mold.

Autumn Leaves Cascade

This cake was created for a fall wedding for a couple who wanted something a little different from traditional flowers on their cake. The gum paste leaves in fall colors make this an unusual yet beautiful change from the ordinary.

Serves 80

12-inch, 8-inch, and 6-inch round cakes, each 4 inches high (2 layers)
1 recipe royal icing
3 recipes gum paste
variety of gum paste leaf cutters
green cloth-covered wires
green florist tape
1 egg white
plastic or marble cutting board
vegetable shortening
X-acto knife
foam rubber
waxed paper
4-inch Styrofoam ball, cut in half
2 7-inch separator plates
4 5-inch columns
2 recipes pure white buttercream
3 recipes rolled fondant
¼-inch wooden dowels
18-inch round foam board base, 3 layers thick
12-inch and 8-inch round foam boards
⅝-inch white ribbon to cover edge of board
brown, orange, red, yellow, and green paste food coloring
tips #19 and #68

In advance:

Prepare the 18-inch base by covering it with thinned white royal icing, as described in the section on cake boards (pages 25–26). When the icing has dried, glue the ribbon around the unfinished edge of the board.

Make the gum paste and divide it into five equal portions. Tint each portion a different color: orange, yellow, brown, green, and deep rust (using brown, red, and orange). Place the paste in plastic bags and let it set, in an airtight container at room temperature, for twenty-four hours.

Using the orange gum paste, first make the bittersweet clusters on wires. Cut the wire into pieces 2½ inches long. Twist four wires together at the bottom, leaving 1 inch of each wire free at the top. Make fifteen of these groupings. Do the same using five wires and make fifteen of these. Make a small hook on the loose ends of all of the wires in each cluster. Roll the gum paste into pea-sized balls. Brush the hooked end of each wire with egg white and insert the wire halfway into the ball. When you have finished a cluster, insert the twisted ends of the wires into a piece of Styrofoam so that the clusters can dry upright. Let these dry for twenty-four hours. Wrap the ends of the wires in green florist tape.

Roll out the different colors of gum paste on a board covered with shortening and cut out leaves. (If you are not able to find a variety of leaf cutters, you can use real leaves as templates. Lay the leaf on a piece of cardboard and cut around the edges with a sharp knife.) Cut out only a few leaves at a time so that they

won't dry out. While you are working, you can place the rest of the unused portion of gum paste under a glass to keep it from drying out.

After cutting out a leaf, place it on a piece of foam rubber and score with a toothpick to make the veins. Place the finished leaves on a surface covered with smooth paper towels. Curl the leaves slightly before they dry to give them a natural look. (See the directions for the holly leaves in the Holly Cake, page 90.)

To give the leaves a more natural coloring, you can knead two of the colors of gum paste together slightly. This will give the leaves a marbled appearance.

Allow all of the leaves to dry for at least twenty-four hours.

To make the top and center decorations, glue one of the 4-inch Styrofoam ball halves to the center of the bottom separator plate with some royal icing. Place the columns in the pegs provided. Place the other half of the Styrofoam ball on a piece of waxed paper, the same size as the bottom of the ball. Then place the ball, with the paper attached, on a larger piece of waxed paper. Insert some of the bittersweet clusters

into each ball. Tint some royal icing green and pipe leaves around the bases of the bittersweet ends, using the #68 tip. Add leaves and more bittersweet to each ball, until the ball is completely covered, securing each with the royal icing. Let these dry for at least twenty-four hours.

To decorate the cake:

Bake all of the cakes and cool. Place each cake on its respective board with a dab of buttercream. Add filling and the top layer. Ice each tier with buttercream and then cover with rolled fondant.

Insert the dowels and stack the tiers on the base as described in the section on tiered cakes (page 26–28). Pipe a shell border around the base of each tier with white buttercream, using the #19 tip.

Insert the bittersweet clusters in the cake, randomly spaced. Attach the leaves to the cake with small dabs of royal icing to hold them in place. Place the top decoration on the 6-inch tier with a dab of buttercream.

Chintz Cake

The design of this cake was inspired by the chintz pattern on the fabric used for the table-cloths at the wedding. Matching the peonies and the colors of the cloth was a challenge, but the results turned out to be quite successful.

Serves 180

Cakes:

15-inch round, 4 inches high (2 layers)
12-inch round, 4 inches high (2 layers)
9-inch round, 4 inches high (2 layers)
7-inch round, 3 inches high
4-inch round, 3 inches high

Flowers:

20 pink gum paste peonies on wires
20 large white and pale yellow double-layered daisies (page 15)
15 small pale purple double-layered daisies (page 15)
25 purple petunias (pages 18–19)
50 small white, pink, and purple daisies (page 15)
40 light and dark green toothpick leaves (pages 20–21)

3-inch Styrofoam ball, cut in half
2 8-inch separator plates
4 4-inch columns
waxed paper
22-inch round foam board, 3 layers thick
⅝-inch-wide white ribbon
5 recipes off-white rolled fondant
5 recipes pure white basic buttercream icing
15-inch, 12-inch, 9-inch, and 4-inch round foam boards
¼-inch wooden dowels

violet and raspberry powdered colors
tips #3, #66, #70, #199

In advance:

Make the gum paste peonies.

1 recipe gum paste
small, medium, and large rose petal cutters
1¼-inch round cutter
20 3-inch lengths of green heavy-gauge cloth-covered wire
green florist tape
1 egg white, slightly beaten
small paintbrush
small rolling pin
plastic or marble cutting board
vegetable shortening
large piece of 1-inch-thick Styrofoam, 12 inches square

Make the gum paste and let it rest for twenty-four hours at room temperature, tightly wrapped in plastic. Then, tint half of the paste a deep pink and add a little green to soften the color. If the paste gets sticky, knead in some of the dry paste mixture.

Take a 3-inch piece of wire and bend the tip to form a small hook. Needlenose pliers work best for this (Figure 1). Form a ½-inch ball of gum paste. Dip the hooked end of the wire in the egg white and shake off the excess. Insert the wire halfway into the ball (Figure 2). Insert the other end of the wire into a piece of Styrofoam to allow it to dry in an upright position. Make twenty of these and let them dry overnight.

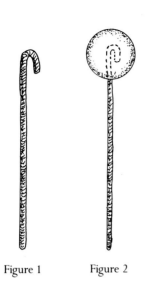

Figure 1   Figure 2

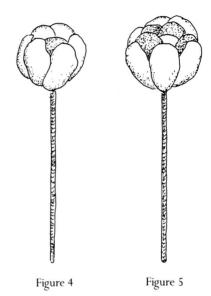

Figure 4   Figure 5

You will need four gum paste cutters to make the peonies (Figure 3). After the gum paste balls have dried, cover the cutting board with a thin coating of shortening. Roll out a small amount of pink gum paste on the cutting board. Roll the paste out as thin as possible. Cut out six petals with the smallest petal cutter.

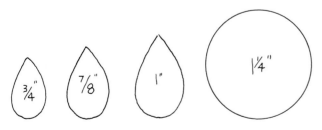

Figure 3

Pick up one of the petals from the board and place a glass upside-down over the rest of the petals to keep them from drying out. Gum paste dries very quickly, so the petals must be kept pliable while you are working. Rub a little of the dry gum paste mixture in the palm of

one hand. Place the petal in your palm and flatten the round edge of the petal with the tip of a finger. Dip a small paintbrush in the egg white and brush onto the dried ball of gum paste. Press the pointed end of the petal to the ball and curve the petal in toward the center of the ball. Place all six of the petals on the ball, overlapping each petal (Figure 4). Set the wire in a piece of Styrofoam to dry. Add the first six petals to all twenty of the gum paste balls.

By the time you have placed the small petals on all of the flowers, the first petals you made will be dry enough for you to continue adding the next row of petals. The next six petals are made with the medium-sized rose cutter in the same manner as the small petals (Figure 5).

When all of the flowers have twelve petals, add six more medium-sized petals, still curving the petals inward (Figure 6). Since the weight of all the petals may force them to fall, the flowers should now be dried upside down. Place the Styrofoam on the end of a table and place a book on the foam to keep it from falling. Place

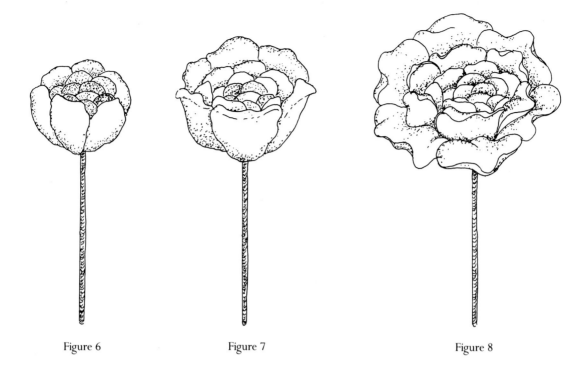

Figure 6   Figure 7   Figure 8

the stems of the flowers in the bottom of the foam. Let the flowers dry overnight before adding more petals.

Add six more petals using the large rose cutter and curve the tips of the petals away from the center (Figure 7). Allow these to dry upside down while making the other flowers.

The last six petals are made with a round cutter. Flatten the entire outer rim of the circle in the palm of your hand. These petals should again be curved outward (Figure 8). Let the entire flower dry right-side up for at least twenty-four hours. Cover the wires with green florist tape.

Next, set one half of the 3-inch Styrofoam ball in the center of the 8-inch separator plate. Use a little royal icing to hold the ball in place. Set the four columns in the pegs on the plate. Place the other half of the ball on a piece of waxed paper, securing it with a dab of royal icing.

Place ten small and five large flowers and half of the toothpick leaves in the Styrofoam, piping

royal icing leaves with the #70 tip between the flowers and leaves as you work. Set these aside to dry for twenty-four hours.

Cover the surface of the 22-inch board with thinned white royal icing. Let it dry completely. Glue a ribbon around the edge of the board.

Make all of the rolled fondant and wrap in plastic wrap. Place it in an airtight container at room temperature for twenty-four hours.

To decorate the cake:

Bake all of the cakes and cool them completely. Place each filled tier, except for the 7-inch tier, on a foam board with a dab of buttercream to hold in place. Place the 7-inch tier on the top separator plate. Cover each tier with a coat of buttercream and then cover each tier with rolled fondant.

Insert wooden dowels into tiers as described in the section on tiered cakes (pages 26–28).

Cover the surface of each tier with a filigree pattern using white buttercream and the #3

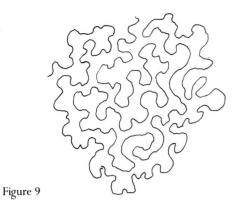

Figure 9

tip. The filigree is a continuous squiggly line of icing that does not overlap (Figure 9).

Pipe a large shell border around the base of each tier with white buttercream and the #199 tip.

Pipe green buttercream stems with the #3 tip randomly around the tiers. Pipe a few green leaves along the stems, using the #66 tip. Press small daisies into the wet buttercream at the base of the leaves.

Pipe randomly placed green buttercream leaves with the #70 tip around the base of each tier. Insert the rest of the large peonies in the cake at the base of the leaves. Place the rest of the flowers on the cake, piping more green leaves next to the flowers to hold them in place.

Carefully remove the top bouquet from the waxed paper. Place a 3-inch circle of waxed paper on the top of the cake with a little buttercream. Place a dab of buttercream on top of the waxed paper and attach the bouquet to the top of the cake.

Precious Wedding Gifts

I created this cake for Bride's *magazine. Gold and silver make this a very special cake for a special occasion. Don't worry; the gold and silver are completely edible.*

Serves 125

Cakes:

12-inch square, 4 inches high (2 layers)
9-inch square, 4 inches high (2 layers)
6-inch square, 3½ inches high (2 layers)

1 recipe royal icing
16-inch square foam board, 3 layers thick
⅝-inch-wide white ribbon
white glue
1 recipe gum paste
sugar mold box, made from a 3½-inch box and lid
6 large rubber bands
tape measure
silver, gold, and white iridescent edible powders
lemon extract
silver and gold dragees, in assorted sizes
waxed paper
12-inch, 9-inch, and 6-inch square foam boards
3 recipes rolled fondant
3 recipes white buttercream icing
¼-inch wooden dowels
pattern tracing wheel
1-inch-wide metal ruler
plastic 30-60-90 degree triangle
1 package 22-karat gold leaf (available in art supply stores)
½-inch-wide flat, soft paintbrush
clear piping gel
tips #1, #7, #60, #61

In advance:

Cover the 16-inch base with thinned white royal icing. Let the board dry for twenty-four hours. Glue the white ribbon around the edge when the icing is dry.

Make the gum paste and place it in a plastic bag. Set it in an airtight container. Let it set for twenty-four hours at room temperature.

Next, make the sugar mold box for the top of the cake. Take a 3½-inch box and lid and slice open the corners using a sharp knife (Figure 1). Make sure that the insides are clean and have no ragged edges. Close the box and lid back into their original position and secure with the rubber bands (Figure 2). Mix the sugar and water as directed in the section on sugar molds

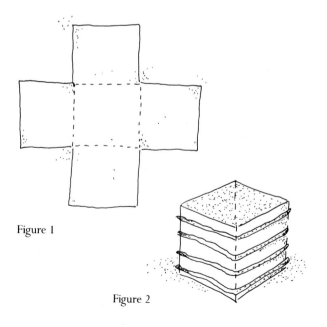

Figure 1

Figure 2

138

(pages 9–10). Press the sugar into the box and lid until fully packed and level off the tops. Carefully remove the rubber bands and gently pull back the sides of the box and the lid. Do not remove the molds from the boxes until the sugar has set for twenty-four hours. Then remove the molds from the boxes and hollow out the inside of the large mold. Let this mold dry upright. Turn the lid upside down onto a paper towel to dry completely. Let them dry for twenty-four more hours.

When the sugar molds are dry, place the lid mold on top of the box mold with a little royal icing. Lay a tape measure on the box and measure from the base, up the side, across the top, and down the opposite side. Roll out two strips of gum paste ½ inch wide by the measurement from the tape measure. Lightly brush the paste with water and lay the damp side down across the mold on each side. Let the paste dry overnight.

When the gum paste strips are dry, paint them with a little gold powder mixed with lemon extract. (Use about ¼ teaspoon of powder to a few drops of extract.)

Pipe dots of white royal icing on the sugar mold, using the #1 tip, and place small silver and gold dragees in the icing. Cover the mold with dragees in a random pattern.

Next, pipe the loops for the bows. Pipe loops onto waxed paper with white royal icing using the #60 tip for the small loops and the #61 tip for the larger loops. Pipe twenty small loops, about 1½ inches long, for the top bow and twenty-five 2-inch loops for the larger bow. It's a good idea to make extra in case some break. Set these aside to dry for twenty-four hours.

When the loops are dry, paint the small loops with gold powder mixed with a little lemon extract. The lemon extract evaporates quickly, so you may have to add more while you are working. Paint the larger loops with white iridescent powder and lemon extract.

Make the small gold bow on the top of the sugar mold as directed in the section on icing bows (page 21). Use white royal icing to form the bow. When the bow is dry, carefully paint the white icing with the gold powder mixture.

When the loops are dry, make the large white gum paste bow for the bottom layer as directed in the section on gum paste bows (pages 22–23). Set on a paper towel to dry for at least two days.

When the bow is dry, paint it with white iridescent powder and lemon extract. Then paint a silver stripe along the center of the ribbons and the bow ends. Paint a silver stripe in the other direction across the center of the bow. Use silver powder mixed with lemon extract.

Pipe royal icing dots on either side of the silver stripes on the gum paste bow, using the #1 tip. Pipe dots along the outer edges of the bow and ribbons.

To make the silver ellipses for the bottom layer, take about ½ cup white royal icing and thin with water until a drop of icing disappears into the rest of the icing on the count of 10. Using the #1 tip, pipe ½-inch-long ovals onto a sheet of waxed paper. You will need about one hundred ovals. Allow these to dry overnight.

When the ellipses are dry, paint them with silver powder mixed with a little lemon extract.

Make all of the rolled fondant and let it set, wrapped in plastic in an airtight container, for twenty-four hours at room temperature.

To decorate the cake:

Bake all of the cakes and let them cool. Set each tier on its respective board. Place the 12-inch tier on the 16-inch board. Cover the bottom tier with white buttercream. Roll out a piece of fondant and cut a 14-inch square. Carefully lay the fondant square on top of the

12-inch tier, with 1 inch hanging over each edge. Smooth the fondant over the corners with your hands. Place dowels in the cake for support as directed in the section on tiered cakes (pages 26–28).

Cover the 9-inch tier with buttercream and then cover with rolled fondant. To quilt the fondant, place a 1-inch-wide ruler diagonally across the top of the cake, lining up one edge of the ruler with the two opposite corners of the cake. Run the serrated tracing wheel along both edges of the ruler, making two dotted lines. Move the ruler over and line the ruler up with the dotted line and make another dotted line, parallel to the first one. Cover the top of the cake with parallel lines.

Turn the cake and line up the ruler with the two other corners. Make dotted lines, crisscrossing the first set of lines at a right angle. The top of the cake will now be covered with 1-inch squares.

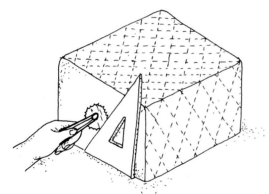

Figure 3

The quilt lines on the side of the cake line up with the lines on the top. Place a triangle against the side of the cake and line up the angled edge of the triangle with a line on the top of the cake. Run the tracing wheel along the angle (Figure 3). Move the triangle over to line up with the next line on the top and continue making lines on the side of the cake. Re-peat this procedure on all sides of the cake.

Turn the angle to face the opposite way and trace lines in the other direction.

When all of the quilt lines are made, you are ready to add the gold leaf.

Draw an outline of the bottom of the 6-inch pan in the center of the top of the 9-inch tier with a toothpick. It is not necessary to put gold leaf in this area. Insert dowels into the 9-inch tier within the 6-inch outline.

Brush one side of the quilted tier with a little water. Carefully press a sheet of gold leaf against the wet fondant. Hold the gold sheets by the paper backing. The gold will disintegrate if you try to pick it up with your hands. If the gold does not completely stick, gently brush down the gold with a small, dry brush. Don't worry if the gold buckles a little. The overall effect will still be beautiful. Cover all of the sides and the top, up to the 6-inch outline, with gold. If the gold does not stick in a small area, brush the fondant with a small amount of water and add a small piece of gold to the spot. Place this tier on top of the 12-inch tier.

Before placing the 6-inch tier on the 9-inch tier, you need to add the silver stripes to the 6-inch square. Cover the 6-inch square with a smooth coat of white buttercream. Place the tier on a piece of waxed paper. Place the triangle next to the side of the cake, but not touching. Starting at the bottom of the left side of the cake, make a toothpick line up the side of the cake, using the long angled edge as your guide. Continue making diagonal lines, 1 inch apart, along the side of the cake (Figure 4). Turn the cake clockwise, and mark the next side with diagonal lines *facing the opposite direction* (Figure 5).

Turn the cake again and mark the sides as in Figure 4. Turn the cake again and mark the sides as in Figure 5.

Mark the top of the cake by connecting the lines from the sides (Figure 6).

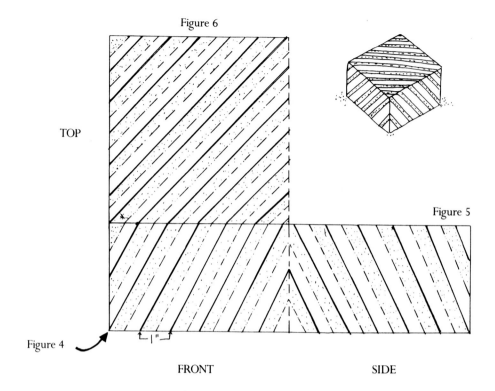

Figure 6

TOP

Figure 5

Figure 4

FRONT   SIDE

Roll out a piece of fondant ⅛ inch thick and cut three 15x¼-inch strips. Pipe a thin line of buttercream on the back of each strip. This will help it adhere to the cake. Lay the strips on the top of the cake and then press along the sides of the cake, using the toothpick marks as a guide for one edge of the strip. Cut ten more strips the same width and decreasing in length and lay on the cake in the same manner. Cut off the excess fondant at the bottom edge.

Place the striped tier on top of the quilted tier. Insert a dowel into the center of the 6-inch tier to support the sugar mold.

Carefully paint the stripes on the 6-inch tier with the silver and lemon mixture.

To make the remaining ribbons, knead together the remaining rolled fondant and gum paste. Roll out the fondant mixture and cut four strips, each 5½ inches long by 1 inch

wide. Brush the back of a strip with water and place it on the front of the bottom tier, to the left of the center. Place the second strip on the back of the bottom tier, across from the first strip. Place the next two strips on the sides of the bottom tier.

Paint with white iridescent powder and then paint silver stripes down the center of all of the ribbons and, using the #1 tip, royal icing dots to match the gum paste bow.

Cut two strips of the fondant mixture, each ½ inch wide by 15 inches long. Brush with water and set on the 9-inch tier diagonally across the sides. Place the second strip on the opposite side of the tier. Use the photograph as a guide.

Using the #7 tip, pipe a dot border with white buttercream along the bottom of the 12-inch tier.

Attach the silver ellipses in a random pattern to the bottom of the 12-inch tier. Pipe a small dot of buttercream to the back of the ellipse and press into the tier. Place gold dragees randomly around the ellipses. Cover the rest of the surface with small buttercream dots.

Mix ¼ cup of the piping gel with ¼ teaspoon of silver powder. Pipe vertical stripes with the #1 tip from the bottom of the quilted tier and down the fondant-covered area on the top of the 12-inch tier.

Using the #7 tip, pipe a dot border along the bottom edges of the 9-inch and 6-inch tiers with buttercream.

Place large silver dragees at the intersections of the lines on the quilted tier, piping small dots of buttercream to hold them in place.

Pipe a mound of white royal icing in the upper right hand corner of the quilted tier and set the large loops to form a bow.

Place the sugar mold on the top of the cake and place the gum paste bow on the 12-inch tier on top of the ribbon, piping a mound of royal icing to hold the bow in place.

Lilac Garden Cake

The lilac color of this cake offsets the multitude of white flowers surrounding the edges. Once you have made all of the flowers, the rest of the cake is easy!

Serves 170

Cakes:

8-inch round, 2½ inches high (2 layers)
12-inch round, 3 inches high (2 layers)
16-inch round, 4 inches high (2 layers)

Flowers:

50 white toothpick roses, carnations, and daisies
   (pages 15–16)
30 white grape clusters on wires
230 white roses, daisies, and carnations (pages
   15–16)
200 white grape clusters
15 large white double-layer daisies (page 15)
40 pale green wired leaves (pages 20–21)

1 recipe royal icing
waxed paper
white cloth-covered wires
1 sugar mold vase, 3 inches high by 3½ inches
   wide
2 3-inch Styrofoam balls
22-inch round foam board, 3 layers thick
⅝-inch-wide white ribbon
15-inch, 12-inch, and 8-inch round foam boards
4 recipes pure white buttercream icing
icing comb
¼-inch wooden dowels
moss green and purple paste food coloring
tips #2, #4, #5, #17, #65, #68, #70

In advance:

Make all of the flowers and leaves. To make the grape clusters, place a sheet of waxed paper on a flat surface. Fit a #4 tip onto a bag filled with white royal icing. Pipe a dot, and let the icing drag to form a point. Pipe two more dots below the first dot (Figure 1). Then add three more dots (Figure 2). Pipe two more dots to finish (Figure 3). Make larger clusters with the #5 tip, adding five more dots to the cluster. Make two hundred of these clusters of grapes.

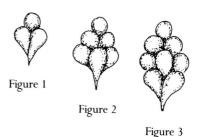

Figure 1

Figure 2

Figure 3

To make the grapes on wires, make the grapes in the same manner as described above, but insert the end of a 5-inch wire into the pointed end of the cluster, halfway into the cluster, while the icing is wet. When all of the clusters are dry, turn over the wired clusters and pipe grapes on the back. Make thirty wired grape clusters.

Make the sugar mold (see pages 9–10) and let it dry overnight. Then hollow out the top

Figure 4

enough to fit the bottom half of a 3-inch Styrofoam ball. Let the mold dry completely.

Cut the other Styrofoam ball in half. Then, cut off the top third of one half. This will form the base for your sugar mold. Glue the sugar mold to the Styrofoam base using a dab of royal icing (Figure 4).

Place the mold on a piece of waxed paper and, using the #17 tip, pipe lilac-colored royal icing lines vertically up the surface of the vase and base. Pipe a shell border around the bottom of the base, at the intersection of the base and vase, and around the top edge. Let this dry for twenty-four hours.

When the vase has dried completely, you can start inserting your flowers, grapes, and leaves into the top Styrofoam ball. Cover the surface of the ball with white royal icing from tip #17 as you insert the flowers.

Cover the 22-inch foam board base with thinned lilac-colored royal icing and allow it to dry for at least twenty-four hours. Glue the ribbon around the edge of the base.

To decorate the cake:

Bake all of the cakes and allow them to cool completely. Place each tier on its respective foam board with a dab of buttercream and filling in between the layers. Cover the tiers with a thin layer of lilac buttercream. When the thin layer of icing is dry, generously ice each tier with softened lilac buttercream and comb the icing up the sides vertically, using the icing comb. Clean the comb after each vertical stroke.

Insert dowels into the tiers and stack the tiers on the prepared board as directed in the section on tiered cakes (pages 26–28).

Pipe green stems with the #2 tip randomly all around the icing-covered base. Pipe stems halfway down each tier. Start placing the largest flowers around the cake and base, using green buttercream and the #70 tip to set them in place. Set the smaller flowers and grape clusters around the cake in the same manner. Leave enough room on the top tier for the vase of flowers.

After all of the flowers and grapes are in place, go back with a darker green buttercream and pipe leaves in between the flowers, using the #65 and #68 tips. Pipe #65 leaves along the stems.

Finally, place the vase on a piece of round waxed paper the same size as the base and attach to the top of the cake with a dab of buttercream.

Gothic Cathedral Cake

This elegant cake was inspired by the window arches in a Gothic cathedral. Carefully constructed run-in sugar panels give it a medieval feeling.

It is very important to be extremely exacting when measuring and piping the various components of this cake. Otherwise, all of the parts may not fit together as planned and the visual effect of the cake will be lost.

Serves 75

Cakes:

12-inch round, 2 inches high (2 layers)
6-inch round, 4½ inches high (2 layers)
6-inch half ball

3 recipes royal icing
waxed paper
16⅝-inch round foam board, 3 layers thick
⅝-inch-wide yellow ribbon
6-inch, 7¼-inch, and 13-inch round foam boards
X-acto knife
1 recipe buttercream icing
2 recipes rolled fondant
¼-inch wooden dowels, or plastic drinking straws
5-inch metal or plastic triangle
tape measure
purple, yellow, brown, and pink food coloring
tips #2, #3, #7, #18

In advance:

Prepare the run-in sugar design for the base by dividing the board into sixteen equal sections as follows. Draw the outline of the board on a piece of paper. Fold the paper into sixteen equal sections. Unfold the paper and place it over the board. Mark each section with a pinhole through the paper into the board. Make a pinhole in the center of the paper. Draw pencil lines connecting the dots through the center of the circle to the opposite side. Make a mark on each of the sixteen lines, ¼ inch in from the outer edge of the board (Figure 1).

Using the pattern provided (Figure 2), place

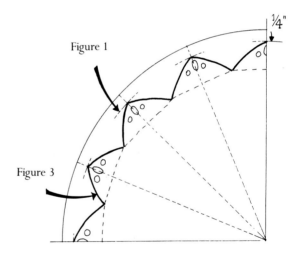

Figure 1

Figure 3

¼"

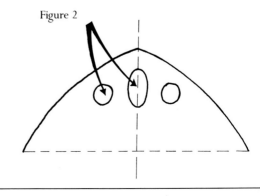

Figure 2

147

the tip of the arch for the board design at the ¼ inch mark. Line up the center line of the arch with the line on the board and outline the arch on the board with a pencil line. Draw the three circles inside each arch (Figure 3).

Make 3 recipes of royal icing. It is important to tint all of the icing at one time, since it would be difficult to achieve identical coloring later. Tint 1½ recipes of the icing pale yellow, adding a tiny amount of brown to soften the color. Tint 1 recipe pink and add a touch of purple. The rest of the white icing will be added to the pink after the board has been iced.

Pipe a yellow outline of all of the arches onto the board, using the #3 tip. Outline the three circles in the center of the arches (at arrows on Figure 2).

Thin 1½ cups of the yellow icing with water until it reaches the consistency of thin syrup. (See the section on run-in sugar, page 8.) Using the #3 tip and the thinned icing, fill in the arches inside the outlines and fill in the entire center section of the board. Let it dry overnight.

Thin ¾ cup of pink icing and fill in the outer edge of the board around the arches with the #3 tip. Pipe pink icing in the center of the circles in the arches. Set aside and let it dry completely.

When the board has dried, with a #3 tip and stiff yellow icing, pipe an outline around each arch and all of the circles. Glue the ribbon around the edge of the board.

To make the run-in sugar arches, use the patterns provided (Figures 4 and 5). You will need to make eight large arches and sixteen small arches, although it's a good idea to make a few extra in case of breakage. Trace the patterns on a piece of paper and place a piece of waxed paper over them. Tape down the waxed paper. On the waxed paper, outline each arch with stiff yellow royal icing, using the #3 tip. Fill in each arch with thinned yellow royal icing

piped from the #3 tip. Let these dry for twenty-four hours.

Take the remaining pink royal icing and mix it with the remaining white royal icing to make it a pale pink. After the arches have dried, outline them with a #2 tip and stiff pink icing. Outline all of the details on the arches. Work very carefully, because any flaw in the outlines will be obvious. Pipe dots where indicated on the pattern (at arrow on Figure 5). Set these aside to dry for a few hours.

The boards that will be placed below each tier must also be made with extreme precision. Outline a 7¼-inch circle on a piece of paper and divide the circle into eight equal sections. Draw a straight line between the end of each of the eight sections (Figure 6). Measure the distance between each section along these lines and check the measurements of the base of the large arches. These measurements should be the same. Adjust the lines on the octagon to match the arches. Cut off the rounded end of each section. Place the paper pattern on top of a

Figure 4

7¼-inch foam board and cut out the shape. Transfer the markings on the paper to the board with a pin.

Make a 13-inch circle of foam board and divide it into sixteen sections. Repeat the same procedure as for the 7¼-inch octagon, making a sixteen-sided board (Figure 7).

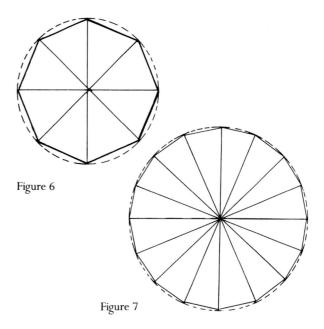

Figure 6

Figure 7

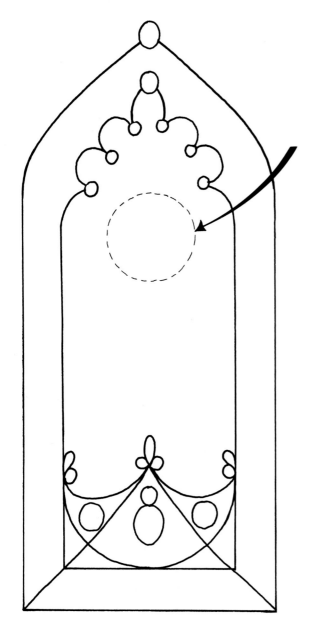

Figure 5

Make the pale yellow rolled fondant, wrap it in plastic and seal it in an airtight container, and let it set overnight at room temperature.

To decorate the cake:

Bake the cakes and cool them completely. Place the bottom 12-inch layer on the 13-inch, sixteen-sided board, using a dab of buttercream to hold it in place. Add filling and cover with buttercream. Place the rolled fondant on the cake. Place dowels in the center of the cake as described in the section on tiered cakes (pages 26–28).

Place the 6-inch layer on the 7¼-inch octagon. Add filling and cover with buttercream. Cover with the fondant. Place the half ball cake on the 6-inch board. Cover with buttercream and fondant. Set the ball on top of the 6-inch layer, securing it with a dab of buttercream.

Place a large metal or plastic triangle against the 6-inch cake at the point of the tip of one section of the octagon and parallel to the side of the cake. Score a vertical line up the side of the cake with a toothpick (Figure 8). Repeat this step all around the cake.

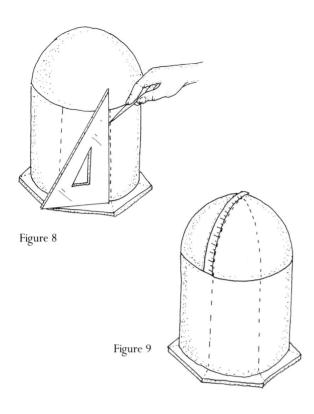

Figure 8

Figure 9

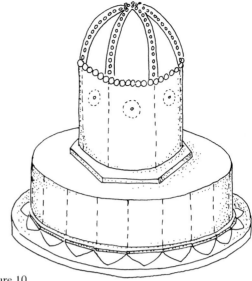

Figure 10

Repeat this procedure on the large tier, making sixteen divisions.

Place a tape measure over the top of the cake, matching up the vertical lines on opposite sides of the cake. Draw a toothpick line across the dome and divide the dome into eight equal sections (Figure 9).

Pipe small pink royal icing dots along the lines on the dome with the #2 tip. Pipe parallel lines on either side of the line of dots, just slightly away from the dots.

Pipe larger dots along the division between the 6-inch dome and the 6-inch cake to hide the foam board.

Mark the outline of the circle in the center of each large arch on the cake as indicated on Figure 5, at arrow. Pipe a thin outline around the circle with the #2 tip and pink royal icing. Pipe a large dot in the center of each circle.

Center the 6-inch tier on top of the 12-inch tier, securing it with a dab of buttercream. The flat side of the octagon should be centered between a scored vertical line on the 12-inch tier (Figure 10).

Remove the large run-in arches from the waxed paper by carefully sliding a metal spatula under the length of each arch. Pipe a thick line of stiff yellow royal icing with the #18 tip along the top edge of one section of the octagon board and up either side of the cake section, stopping just below the division of the dome and the 6-inch tier. Carefully place a large arch up against the icing, at right angles to the board. Place all of the large arches around the cake. Pipe large yellow royal icing dots around the base of the octagon, using the #7 tip.

Place the sixteen small arches around the bottom tier in the same manner as the large arches. Pipe large yellow dots around the base of the 12-inch tier.

To complete the cake, with a #7 tip pipe a large cone on the top of the dome with yellow royal icing. Pipe concentric circles around the dome, using less pressure on the pastry bag as you move toward the tip. Pipe pink dots around the base of the cone, the circles of the cone, and one dot on the top.

The Lace Cake

Ribbons of tulle decorated with royal icing make this cake very feminine and delicate. It was created to match the lace bows on the bride's gown.

Serves 200

15-inch, 12-inch, 10-inch, 8-inch, and 6-inch round cakes, 3 inches high (2 layers)

Flowers

35 large white toothpick lilies (page 18)
50 assorted white and pink toothpick roses and daisies (pages 15–16)
40 clusters of baby's breath (page 19)
50 wired white leaves (pages 20–21)

3½-inch-wide sugar mold
2 3-inch Styrofoam balls, one cut in half
half of a 6-inch Styrofoam ball
2 recipes royal icing
waxed paper
2 11-inch separator plates
2 7-inch separator plates
6 5-inch columns
4 3-inch columns
20-inch round foam board base, 3 layers thick
⅝-inch white ribbon to cover the edge of the board
15-inch, 12-inch, and 8-inch round foam boards
½ yard stiff white tulle
4 recipes white buttercream icing
6 recipes rolled fondant
¼-inch wooden dowels
5 pieces of white cloth-covered wire
white florist tape
tips #2, #13, #32, #65

In advance:

Make all of the flowers and leaves. Allow two days to dry.

Make the sugar mold. Before the mold dries completely, hollow out the top to fit a 3-inch Styrofoam ball. Let the mold dry completely. Insert the ball into the hollow of the mold, using a little royal icing to secure it in place.

Cover the ball with the toothpick flowers and leaves, piping white royal icing with the #32 tip over the surface of the ball to hold the flowers in place.

Place the sugar mold on a piece of waxed paper and pipe a royal icing star border around the base, using a #32 tip. Let this dry for twenty-four hours.

Attach half of a 6-inch Styrofoam ball to the 11-inch separator plate with royal icing. Fit four 5-inch columns onto the plate in the designated posts and glue two more columns in between the columns on the right and left sides, using royal icing. Cover the ball with toothpick flowers and leaves and cover the surface of the ball with royal icing, making sure that the height of the flowers is not above the height of the columns. Do the same with the halved 3-inch ball on the 7-inch separator plate. Add the 3-inch columns to the pegs.

To make the decorated tulle, cut six strips of tulle, 2 inches wide by 36 inches long. Tape each strip to a piece of waxed paper slightly wider and longer than the tulle. Do not stretch the tulle when you tape it down. Thin one cup

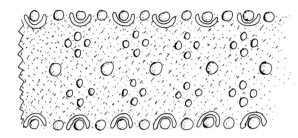

Figure 1

of royal icing slightly with a few drops of water. If royal icing is too stiff, it will not adhere to the tulle. Pipe the lace pattern with the #2 tip along the entire length of the tulle (Figure 1). Lay the strips on a flat surface to dry. When it is time to use the tulle, carefully pull the waxed paper away from the tulle. Don't worry if some pieces of icing come off the tulle; it will not change the effect of the lace pattern.

Cover the three-layer 20-inch board with thinned white royal icing. When the icing is dry, glue the white ribbon around the edges of the board.

Make all of the fondant one day in advance. Wrap it securely in plastic and place it in an airtight container.

To decorate the cake:

Bake all of the cakes and let them cool. Set the 15-inch, 12-inch, and 8-inch cakes on each foam board of the designated size, with filling in between the layers. Set the 10-inch and 6-inch cakes on the separator plates. Cover with buttercream, and then cover with fondant. Stack the cakes according to directions for tiered cakes, inserting dowels into the tiers as supports (pages 26–28).

Pipe a star border around the base of each layer with the #32 tip and white buttercream. Pipe #65 white leaves and #13 pink stars randomly around the surface of each tier.

To finish the cake with the tulle ribbons, remove the tulle from the waxed paper. Holding the center of the strip in one hand, make a 3-inch loop to the left (Figure 2) and then another loop to the right of the center (Figure 3), using a figure-eight motion, overlapping the ribbons. Gather the middle of the bow together and twist a length of wire around the center (Figure 4). (The drawings have been simplified to show you the basic movements to use to make the bow.) Twist the ends of the wire together and wrap the wire with white florist tape. Insert the end of the wire into the top of the 6-inch layer. With a pair of scissors, cut off the excess tulle so that the ends are notched. Make a slightly larger bow for the 8-inch tier and let the notched ends trail onto the top of the 10-inch tier. For the 12-inch tier, take a length of tulle and drape it around the front of the cake, letting the ends hang down to the bottom of the cake. Secure the tulle on the left and right sides of the cake with a small U-shaped piece of wire wrapped in florist tape. (Note: Make sure you let the person who is cutting the cake know about these wires.) Make three more bows, with loops 5 inches long, for the sides of the 12-inch layer and the front of the bottom layer. Place the sugar mold on the top of the cake, with a little royal icing to hold it in place.

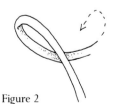

Figure 2

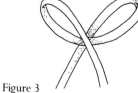

Figure 3

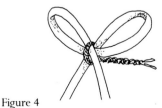

Figure 4

Antique Wedding Cake

The dusty rose, lavender, and blue flowers on this cake give it an antique look. It's the perfect cake for a traditional wedding, but the two butterflies on the top, which symbolize the bride and groom, add a touch of lightheartedness.

Serves 115

14-inch, 10-inch, and 6-inch round cakes, 4 inches high (2 layers)

Flowers:

15 large white lilies (page 18)
15 medium-sized blue delphiniums (page 18)
65 white and lavender roses (pages 15–16)
40 mauve and dusty rose daisies and petunias (pages 15–16, 18–19)
50 clusters of heather on wires (page 19)
50 clusters of Queen Anne's lace on wires
50 green leaves on wires (pages 20–21)
20 blue delphiniums on toothpicks (page 18)
30 white and lavender roses on toothpicks (pages 15–16)
15 large white lilies on toothpicks (page 18)
15 rose and mauve petunias and daisies on toothpicks (pages 15, 18–19)

2 recipes royal icing
green cloth-covered wires
green florist tape
waxed paper
lemon extract
small paintbrush
sugar mold vase, 3½ inches wide by 2¾ inches high
3-inch Styrofoam ball, cut in half
5-inch Styrofoam ball, cut in half
4 5-inch columns
2 8-inch separator plates
18-inch round foam board base, 3 layers thick
3 recipes off-white buttercream icing
14-inch and 10-inch round foam boards
¼-inch wooden dowels
⅝-inch white ribbon to cover the edge of 18-inch board
green, yellow, black, and pink food coloring
tips #2, #4, #15, #17, #21, #68

In advance:

To make the Queen Anne's lace, twist together seven 3-inch lengths of green cloth-covered wire so that about 1 inch of each wire is extending above the twist. Make fifty of these clusters. Pipe a star of green royal icing with the #15 tip on the tip of each of the seven wires in the cluster. Set upright in a piece of Styrofoam to dry. Then, pipe seven dots of white royal icing on each green star with the #2 tip (Figure 1). Wrap the wires with green florist tape.

Figure 1

Make all of the flowers and leaves. Allow them to dry for two days. Wrap the wires of the heather with green florist tape.

Make four pairs of wings for the butterflies in pale yellow run-in sugar (page 8) on waxed paper, using the patterns provided (Figures 2 and 3). Allow these to dry for twenty-four hours. When dry, paint the wings as illustrated

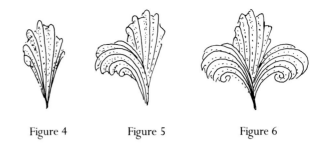

Figure 4   Figure 5   Figure 6

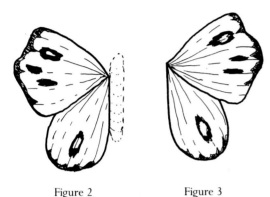

Figure 2   Figure 3

with black coloring mixed with a little lemon extract. When the paint has dried, pipe a line ¾ inch long on a piece of waxed paper for each butterfly, using black royal icing and the #15 tip. Insert a left and a right wing into the icing. Prop the wings up with a ball of Kleenex to dry in a V formation. Let these dry for twenty-four hours.

Make the sugar mold and let it dry for two days. Cut off the top of one of the 3-inch Styrofoam ball halves. Glue the 3-inch Styrofoam ball half to the bottom of the sugar mold with a dab of royal icing. This will serve as the base for the vase. Glue the other half of the ball on top of the mold with a dab of royal icing.

Place the vase on a piece of waxed paper. Using the #17 tip, pipe lines with white royal icing up and down the bottom Styrofoam ball, stopping where the ball meets the sugar mold. Pipe a #17 shell border around the intersection of the base and the vase. Pipe fleur-de-lis shells around the top of the base using the #17 tip

(Figures 4, 5, and 6). Pipe upside-down fleur-de-lis around the top side of the sugar mold. Finish the top edge of the sugar mold with a border of shells (Figure 7). Let this dry for twenty-four hours before adding the flowers.

Insert half of the toothpick flowers and leaves and fifteen of the wired flowers into the Styrofoam ball on the sugar mold, using white royal icing and the #17 tip to hold the flowers in place. Let this dry for twenty-four hours. Glue the two butterflies onto the tops of two of the flowers with a little royal icing. Let these dry in place.

Glue half of the 5-inch Styrofoam ball onto the center of one of the separator plates, using royal icing to hold it in place. Place the columns in the pegs. Insert fifteen of the wired

Figure 7

Figure 8

flowers and the rest of the toothpick flowers and leaves into the ball, using royal icing piped from the #17 tip to secure them in place. Set these aside to dry.

Cover the 18-inch base with thinned royal icing and let it dry for twenty-four hours. Glue the ribbon around the edge of the base.

To decorate the cake:

Bake the cakes and allow them to cool. Fill and ice the layers. Assemble the tiers on the foam boards and separator plates, according to the directions for tiered cakes (pages 26–28).

Divide each tier into four equal sections, using the columns as a guide, making marks for the divisions with a toothpick at the top and bottom of each tier. Starting with the bottom tier, draw a diagonal toothpick line from the front top of the tier to the bottom side of the next division. Continue around the cake until you have four equal triangular shapes. Repeat the same markings on the two other tiers. Pipe a shell outline along the lines of the triangles with the buttercream icing and the #17 tip.

Pipe a filigree pattern in buttercream and the #4 tip in every other triangle on the bottom and 10-inch tiers. On the 6-inch tier, pipe dots within the triangles, using the #4 tip.

Using the #21 tip, pipe a shell border around the base of each layer. Insert a wired heather into the center of the base of each triangle. Place a large white lily in the center of each triangle, below the heather. Use green buttercream and the #68 leaf tip to pipe leaves around each flower and to hold them in place. Add the rest of the flowers around the tiers (Figure 8). Place the sugar mold on top of the cake with a dab of buttercream.

Sources for Cake-Decorating Supplies

Maid of Scandinavia
3244 Raleigh Avenue
Minneapolis, MN 55416-2299
1-800-328-6722

The Cake Plate
104 11th N.E.
East Wenatchee, WA 98801
509-884-1549

The Chocolate Gallery
34 West 22nd Street
New York City, NY 10010
212-675-CAKE

Wilton Industries
2240 West 75th Street
Woodridge, IL 60517
708-963-7100

Country Kitchen
3225 Wells Street
Fort Wayne, IN 46808
219-482-4835

Creative Cutters
561 Edward Avenue
Units 1 & 2
Richmond Hill, Ontario, Canada L4C9W6
416-883-5638

Cake Decorators' Association of South Australia
Secretary, Lorraine Joliffe
Pindari, 12 Sussex Crescent
Morphet Vale, SA 5162

Fer Lewis, Cake Ornament Company
156 Alfred Street
Fortitude Valley
Brisbane 4006

New Zealand

New Zealand Cake Decorators Guild
Secretary, Morag Scott
17 Ranui Terrace
Tawa, Wellington

Decor Cakes
RSA Arcade
435 Great South Road
Otahaha

South Africa

South African Sugarcraft Guild, National Office
1 Tuzla Mews
187 Smit Street
Fairland 2195

Jem Cutters
PO Box 115
Kloof, 3 Nisbett Road
Pinetown 3600

Index